YOUR LIFE
YOUR WAY

Best wishes,

Julie Malnor

YOUR LIFE YOUR WAY

The Essential Guide for Women

Lynn Hull and Julie Molner

Marsh Hall International
Publishing Corporation

Cover Artwork by Amanda J. Thompson-Legg
Cover and Interior Design by Cathy L. Bowman
Photograph of Julie Molner by Larry Martin
Photograph of Lynn Hull by James Hargreaves

First printing 2008

ISBN 978-0-9797864-3-3
LCCN 2007935766

www.essentialguideforwomen.com

Dedication

This book is dedicated to all the fantastic women
who have touched our lives with their zest for living,
and to all the women for whom this book
will spark *their* zest for living!

Contents

Acknowledgments   xi

The Birth of This Book   xiii

Getting Started   1

Section One: *The Time of Your Life*

CHAPTER ONE

The Perfect Time—How Can That Be?   7

CHAPTER TWO

Midlife Crisis—A View on Mortality   19

CHAPTER THREE

Empty Nester—Where Have All My Interests Gone?   27

CHAPTER FOUR

Sandwich Generation—Merely the Filling?   33

CHAPTER FIVE

Retirement and Impending Retirement—With a Flourish   45

CHAPTER SIX

Fitness or Illness—Is There a Choice?   53

CHAPTER SEVEN

Divorce or Death of a Spouse—Phoenix Rising   61

CHAPTER EIGHT

Over the Hill?—So…Who Says?   67

CHAPTER NINE

If Not Now, When?   75

Section Two: *Tapping Into Your Energies*

CHAPTER TEN
What Is Deep Energy?   83

CHAPTER ELEVEN
Physical Energy—Deserving and Serving   97

CHAPTER TWELVE
Spiritual Energy—In Us and Around Us   103

CHAPTER THIRTEEN
Communicative Energy—What Did You Say?   111

CHAPTER FOURTEEN
Values—Your Energy Trigger   125

CHAPTER FIFTEEN
How to "Tap Into"   131

Section Three: **Walk Through the Door**

CHAPTER SIXTEEN
Exploring Change—An Adventure   139

CHAPTER SEVENTEEN
Status Quo—Change Perspectives   143

CHAPTER EIGHTEEN
Courage—Standing Up to the Fear   155

CHAPTER NINETEEN
Endless Possibilities—*You* Are the Only Limit!   169

CHAPTER TWENTY
Why Walk?   179

Section Four: **A Richer Life**

CHAPTER TWENTY-ONE
What Is Richness?   187

CHAPTER TWENTY-TWO
Permission—To Do or Simply Be   197

CHAPTER TWENTY-THREE

Freedom—One of the Greatest Riches We Can Have
in Our Life   205

CHAPTER TWENTY-FOUR

Savor Life—It Tastes Real Good!   213

CHAPTER TWENTY-FIVE

Celebrate—There Are More Reasons Than You Think!   223

Bibliography   233

Other Inspirations: Books, Movies, Websites   235

Book Summary   237

About the Authors   239

Write to the Authors   241

Acknowledgments

Our thanks go to the many female friends and clients who inspired us with their stories and agreed to share them in this book. We are grateful too for the women who were patient enough to read our book in its early stages and give us valuable feedback, ideas, and encouragement. Without them our book would not be complete.

We also thank our friends, families, and all those whom we met along the way for their help, advice, and cheerleading as we embarked and continued on this most interesting journey. They are too numerous to mention by name, yet each one made their own unique contribution.

A special thanks to Kate Deubert, our editor, and Cathy Bowman, our interior and cover designer. We have appreciated not only their professionalism but also their genuine interest in this project.

Last but not least, we acknowledge our dear husbands, Alan Hull and Wayne Molner, for their unfailing love, and our beautiful daughters, Elena Hull and Michelle Molner, for their bright ideas and youthful zest for living. Without their support in so many different ways this book would never have been born.

The Birth of This Book

As we looked at the structure of this book, we realized it follows what has happened to us in our own lives. This is the model we produced.

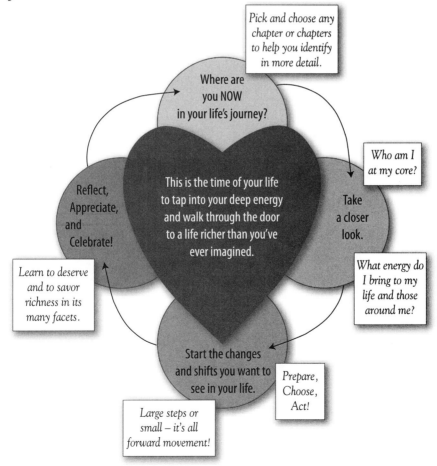

So there we were—Julie in the state of Michigan and Lynn in the UK—total strangers to each other following a similar path unbeknownst to each other. Wanting to live our lives more fully and authentically led us to the same leadership program and eventually collaboration on this book. Through our own period of introspection and change we discovered our shared yearning to let other women experience great shifts in their lives at a time when change seems unlikely or even impossible.

Yes, we experienced fear, hurdles in bringing our dream to fruition—not the least of which was the huge Atlantic Ocean that separates us. How do two different women from essentially different cultures coauthor a book at a great distance? It was understanding and commitment that sustained our determination to bring to the written page a book that coaches and supports other women to live a more fulfilled life. We hope you will enjoy it.

Getting Started

Are you a woman over fifty or approaching fifty with a yearning that hasn't yet been fulfilled? Do you long for things in your life to be different? Or perhaps you know there's more to life and don't know how to get there?

Do you feel this journey we call life has lost a lot of its color—it's too predictable, rather gray? Above all else, don't you just want to create your journey in your own unique way? If so, read on!

> NOW is the time
> YES, right now,
> to create that richer, more satisfying life
> you so deserve!
> No more waiting or putting it off!
> We welcome you in making this period of
> your life extraordinary.

This book is written specifically for you. Why? Because we believe, through our own experiences and growth, and that of many women like us, that this is one of the most precious times of our lives. And yet it can seem to be one of the hardest.

There's so much going on for us women—in our bodies, in our heads, in our own home, work, and family contexts. For some it can feel like being in the midst of a whirlpool. For others it can be quite the opposite: a time when lives are getting emptier, less chaotic.

Wherever you are, if you are right there in the driver's seat, *you* will be the one determining how you want your life to look from now on. There are no rules on this—it's not about doing it "right"— only doing what feels right for you.

With this book as your guide and compass, we invite you to give yourself some time to become curious, daring, and yes, powerful enough to look at your yearnings and suspend self-judgment. You can then consider the choices you want to make and what you might want to leave behind to step fully into who you are. Through the exercises and stories, we coach you step by step to chart the specific course of your journey. We want to jump-start your thought process and ignite or rekindle the fire within you. Are you willing to join us? After all, you just may see your dreams become a reality!

We know some of you will find this prospect exciting, and you may be saying "OK, I'm ready...how do I do it?" Others might be thinking, "Uh-oh, wait a minute, that's a tall order," or perhaps, "Why now...what do you mean?" Whatever you are thinking, we expect you to have questions and reservations. It's part of our natural process trying to keep us safe.

We firmly and passionately believe what we are saying: the time is *now*. And we have much to share about the why, what, when, and how, which we will do as we move through the different sections of this book.

Section One: The Time of Your Life assists you in identifying and claiming who you are at your core, not who you are based on what you do or how others see you. Who we are at our core is much more than what appears on the surface. Rather like an iceberg, there's far more of you that is not visible to others—or even to yourself. We also look at a range of life contexts that may well apply to you. Sometimes several apply at once. You can choose to read all the chapters in this section or only those that apply to you. Gaining clarity on your current situation, your behaviors, beliefs, and attitude will be of great value as you map your course. To get to where you want to go (your goal) we introduce you to the possibility of adjusting your behaviors, beliefs, and attitude.

Section Two: Tapping Into Your Energies invites you to take a deeper look at who you are. We present the different types of energies that naturally reside within you and encourage you to connect with them. There is much more available to you beyond the physical energy that may initially come to mind; there is wisdom, inner knowing or intuition, spiritual and communicative energies. By actively accessing and managing these energies in a way that works for you, you can more easily chart your course and reach your goal.

Section Three: Walk Through the Door coaches you to take the steps necessary to actually set out on your adventure of exploring change, seeing the possibilities. Here you focus on one change you want to see in your life. You will choose a shift that feels right for you—challenging but not overwhelming. We will look at mindsets and perspective and how to work with fear so that you don't get stuck.

Section Four: A Richer Life spells out what we mean by this and gives you the chance to choose how you want to see, savor, and celebrate the richness in your life—not only the big things but also those everyday successes that can go unnoticed. In this section you will be asked to practice giving yourself permission to be who you want to be and to do what makes your heart sing.

To exemplify what we are talking about, throughout the book we share anecdotes about ourselves and other women we know who are extraordinary in their ordinariness. They have all in their different ways jumped in with both feet and taken full responsibility for their lives to experience more joy and fulfillment. We also know they all did their fair share of soul searching and letting go of their previous self-image and limiting beliefs.

There are also exercises, and questions for you to reflect upon, indicated by the icon shown here. Completing these is crucial to making the contents of the book real for you and helping you to reach the change you desire. We suggest you get yourself a separate journal or notebook to record your answers and thoughts as you progress through the book.

There are many ways to use this book:

- Some of you will prefer to read it straight through. If you do, we hope you will return to the questions and exercises—this is where the "juice" is for you!
- If you have already done some personal growth and development work, you may prefer to go straight to the exercises and concentrate on the choices and shifts you want to make.
- For those of you ready for a shift but new to personal growth work, we believe you will get the most benefit from this book by reading and answering the questions and setting aside time to do the exercises as they appear. At various points in the book, you will find it helpful to put the book down and reflect.

Although we believe you will gain from simply reading the book, we encourage you to complete the questions and exercises. They are designed to be developmental and progressive—similar to those we use when coaching clients. If you dedicate the time to do them, they will bring about new insights for you—and there are some very powerful insights awaiting your discovery. You can of course use the book and these exercises over and over again as you continue to make changes and design your life.

The Time of Your Life

Where Are You Now in Your Life's Journey?

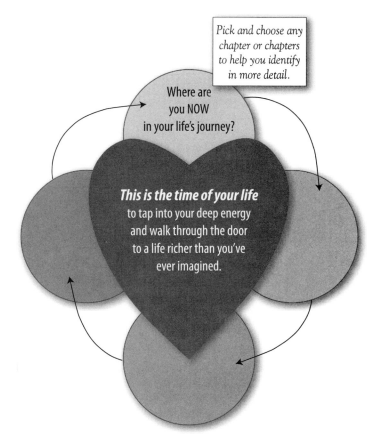

Pick and choose any chapter or chapters to help you identify in more detail.

Where are you NOW in your life's journey?

This is the time of your life to tap into your deep energy and walk through the door to a life richer than you've ever imagined.

The theme of this first section is "The Time of Your Life"—which is something of a play on words. We are pointing to the fact that you are at this "time of your life" (approaching fifty or beyond). Also, we want you to really have "the time of your life" and *now* is the perfect time.

CHAPTER ONE

The Perfect Time— How Can That Be?

How can we say it's the perfect time? Well, for starters, you have grown a great deal as a person through the years and know yourself better now. Therefore, you are better able to make new choices for yourself and venture out in new directions. In other words, this is the time of your life when you are more capable than ever before: maturity is positively on your side!

Next, there is something that only *you* can do, simply because you are unique. We do not intend that to be a glib statement. You genuinely are unique in that you are the only person on this earth who has traveled your journey to get to where you are in your life right now.

Another reason this is a perfect time is that whether we like it or not this is a time of change in our lives, and we are faced with unfamiliar situations. For instance, you may be an "empty nester," in a "midlife crisis," part of the "sandwich generation," and so on. We'll look more closely at these circumstances later, but right now we want to focus on your maturity and uniqueness.

Making the Most of Your Maturity

When you have lived as a woman on Mother Earth as long as you have, we're sure you've been exposed to a great deal...some wonderful experiences and some not so wonderful. You've learned a great deal about what works for you, what doesn't; what satisfies you, what disappoints. Sometimes, however, we don't notice what makes us feel good; we dismiss something because it doesn't fit our concept of how things *should* be. Now's the time to get a sense of who you really are by noticing what has worked for you in the past so that you can use this awareness more effectively today.

Don't hide your light. We assert that you've acquired much more knowledge, wisdom, strengths, and talents than you may recognize. Much of what you know may go unnoticed by you because it seems commonplace; it's such a regular part of you and your life. Take notice. Nothing is commonplace; it all has value.

In your notebook or journal, start a list of all the things you've learned and haven't taken credit for as they surface day to day. Who would benefit from your sharing this wisdom? How much value would there be for you to "make a difference" or "give back," so to speak? As writer Margaret Fuller puts it:

> *If you have knowledge,*
> *let others light their candle at it.*

And remember, since life is a journey, we all continue to learn and grow; it doesn't stop when we hit fifty or indeed any age beyond that! Know that your life can continue to blossom year after year in whatever way feels right for you.

Now that we've got you starting to value your acquired knowledge and talent, there's even more! Creativity can surface in unexpected areas as we mature. Many people think that as we grow older we lose our capability. The truth is our capabilities are changing. For instance, you may be good at gardening but have never tried other types of creative endeavors such as watercolor painting, drawing, singing, or playing a musical instrument. Notice if there is a specific skill or type of artistic work that you are drawn to but have not been able to do in the past, or you believe you're not capable of.

Give it a try…take a class or just play with it, get a feel for it. We aren't saying that you will be good at everything. However we do assert that we all have more talents than we realize. All you need to do is open your mind to the possibility and explore with a playful attitude. You'll have some great surprises awaiting you!

List ten or more things you've wanted to do or try out in your life for which you thought you did not have the talent/skill/patience/opportunity, etc. Please be sure to keep this list handy since you will be referring to it later on in the book.

Your Uniqueness

Now, let's get back to that notion of uniqueness. Just notice how you feel when you read: Your voice is to be heard; you are to be seen. You might respond by saying: "There are other women who know what I know or more. What have I got to offer?" The following quote from author Barbara Sher sums it up quite well:

Every single one of us can do things that no one else can do—can love things that no one else can love.…We are like violins. We can be used for doorstops, or we can make music. You know what to do.

We love this simile likening us to a violin. Indeed we share many qualities. And, in the same way that violins look similar, so we women have common traits. However, no two are ever the same.

Or think of a song you like and imagine different singers you've heard doing their own renditions of it. Not the same, are they? You may prefer one version to another but the point we are making here is the song is sung with the passion of the singer concerned, making each version unique, just like you. Your family, friends, co-workers, your world are waiting for you to show up more with your unique gift. If you choose not to share it, everyone misses out.

This is why it is so critical to attain fulfillment and satisfaction— to live a "rich" life. Does the thought of this sound selfish to you? We aren't talking selfishness here; we're talking self-care, self-love, and love for others. "How so?" you may say. It's quite simple: When we are fulfilled, the best in each one of us surfaces; we have more love, kindness, compassion, and consideration to give to others as well as ourselves. Being satisfied has a positive impact on us…mentally, physically, emotionally, and spiritually. Don't you just feel healthier in every respect when you are happily engaged in what makes your heart sing? Compare it to when you are feeling stuck or thinking you have missed out on some things in life.

Rather like the ripple effect of the pebble in the pond, fulfillment allows us to have a positive impact on everyone we encounter in our daily lives. In a nutshell, the more you are fulfilled, the more your uniqueness shines through, and everyone benefits. Have you ever been in the company of a woman who was so fulfilled and vibrant that her joy was infectious? And what about you? Can you recall having that effect on anyone? Take a few moments to reflect.

Hmmm, maybe you are still thinking negative thoughts about the possibilities here.…Perhaps you are in the land of "I can't," "I shouldn't," or "I mustn't." If so, there is a Shakespearean quote that is totally applicable to what we are saying:

There is nothing either good or bad
but thinking makes it so.…

In other words it is only what we think about something that categorizes it as "good" or "bad" for us. So, we genuinely can look at new possibilities without ruling anything out in the first place on the grounds of "I can't," "I shouldn't," or "I mustn't."

What we need to fully realize is that there are consequences to any choice we make—and we are all able to make the choices and choose the consequences too.

As we are talking about possibilities and change to let more of the real you shine through, to look at fulfilling some of those dreams, to share your uniqueness, we must mention the other people in your life who will be impacted by the changes you make. You may find at first that those closest to you will not all respond favorably. Sometimes this has been the reason for our rejecting change in the past. It can jolt you back into the old way because it feels more comfortable; it causes less disruption.

On the other hand, simply being aware that such reactions from others are normal—that their reactions are about them, not you—is in itself helpful. If you are prepared for opposition, you will be better able to deal with it. So, another of the things we coach you to do in this book is to help you prepare the way for any change, and be able to respond to reactions in a way that serves everyone as well as yourself, while still continuing with your forward movement. Let's face it, family and friends are consciously and unconsciously expecting you to be and live the way you always have; they aren't necessarily ready for you to change, nor will they immediately understand why you are changing and what all of it means. This is the time to be gentle with yourself—and with them too.

In our experience we have friends who have made no changes and appear to be very happy with their lot. However, there is an indication that they are *not* when they say something like "it is not possible," "if only I were younger," or "at my age you can't." They are in some ways envious, in awe, overwhelmed by the changes we have made—either that, or they respond as if we are just plain stupid or "out there."

As time passed and we continued to move forward, our lives have changed.

Lynn:

My circle of friends has changed significantly. I find myself surrounded by people of similar mind—women who are prepared to make a change in the way they see and live their lives. Not all of them are making wild changes, but they are subtly shifting into another gear about their lives. If I were to try to express what makes them different, it's the fact that they are at peace with themselves and eager to make the most of their life in a way that works for them. From what they have said to me, I know that my making the change in some strange way has given them permission to do so too.

I have other friends who have made huge changes in their lives since they approached their fiftieth birthday. One in particular set up her own business and has been extremely successful, earning more in the last couple of years than ever before in her life. Another decided to blow the kids' inheritance on traveling the world (and took her relatively new husband with her). She has seen more than she ever thought possible...and her kids are doing very well without the prospect of their inheritance!

Even my long-time husband who definitely was not into this "personal development" stuff has learned and grown alongside me...and this has happened from a place where I was determined to move forward in my life, even if it meant leaving him behind. I am so pleased that it did not turn out that way, for we now have a much fuller, richer, and more delightful life together.

Julie:

At forty-seven I started a new career in the corporate world without any background in the field. Friends and acquaintances were so shocked to learn I had been hired for the position...they couldn't believe it at my age. Consequently, I learned a great deal and gained more self-confidence and a better understanding of what was missing in my life. That led me to leave the corporate arena at the age of fifty-five so that I could start my coaching practice and explore further in that area. Again friends and co-workers were in awe that I could make such a move at my age. What allowed me to take the steps was the fact that I knew myself better and knew what I was capable of; perhaps I wasn't absolutely sure of what I wanted but I was certain of what I *didn't* want. I knew it was OK to explore and find my way. Women I know tell me they think of me and the things I have done and it helps them to believe they too can make changes; they too are capable of something they didn't believe they could do, especially at their age.

My circle of friends has expanded...I've maintained a connection with some but not all of the friends from my previous career and I have connected with others from various places around the world who are following their calling. I keep learning from everyone.

The moving nature of relationships is perhaps best expressed in the following well-known though unattributed concept of our having three types of friends. There are those who come into our life for a particular reason—to help us through a difficult patch in our life and then, often without warning, they leave our life for it is time for us to move on. They have served the purpose for which they were sent to us. Next are the friends who appear in a particular period or season of our life. They often bring new learning, new happiness, new fulfillment. The friendship will inevitably ebb simply because its time has passed. Then there are the friends we have throughout the whole of our life—the ones who will not leave our life no matter the circumstances, the changes. They bring us life's lessons. These perspectives on friendship certainly help us see that not all people are sent our way for life...and that makes it OK to let go when the time is right.

EXERCISE: So, Who Am I?

There's only one place to start on this journey of discovery and that's with you—a new look at who you are. And we have an exercise to help you do that.

As women we all have various roles—as daughters, wives, mothers, aunts, employees, business owners, etc. Some of us have pretty much lived our lives fulfilling one role, and others have changed roles several times—probably fulfilling several at once!

- *What roles do you perform in life? Circle as many of the roles given on the outside of the diagram as you can, and add any more roles that apply to you. These are just names given to describe the roles you undertake that are understood by society.*

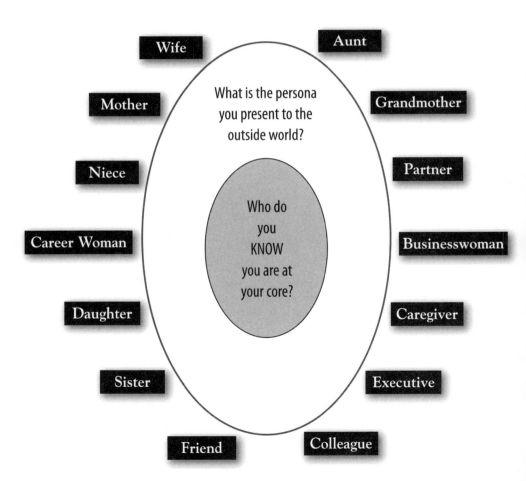

Wife · Aunt · Mother · Grandmother · Niece · Partner · Career Woman · Businesswoman · Daughter · Caregiver · Sister · Executive · Friend · Colleague

What is the persona you present to the outside world?

Who do you KNOW you are at your core?

- *In the outer circle write those words that describe what you think, or you are told, you present to the outside world. This is how you choose to show up in these different roles.*

- *Finally, in the inner circle write as many words as you can that state who you truly are at your core. While there may be some overlap with what you have written in the outer circle, there will always be some additional words that describe the part other people simply do not see. For instance, some people may see you as "stalwart" or "emotionally balanced" while you may feel that words like "old softy" or "happy-go-lucky" or "fun-loving" are the real you and should go in the center.*

- *The big question is how many of those qualities in the innermost circle would you like to show up more overtly in your life? If you are saying to yourself "none," then a curious question to ask yourself is "Where's the resistance?"*

Resistance can come from an unwillingness to let go, or even to look. Sometimes this can be due to disappointments we have had. Perhaps one of the disappointments you are carrying is about unfulfilled dreams.

Living Your Dream

Throughout the various stages of our lives, each one of us has experienced desires and dreams—that special something that stirs within us. For some of us it may have been the desire to become a painter, a singer, a dancer, a business owner, or mother. Others may have dreamed of building a new home, buying property in the country, traveling to exotic locations, getting a job, leaving a job, staying home to cook and garden.

What dreams did you have when you were
a child, teen, or in earlier years?
Have you followed those dreams?
If not, what stopped you?

Many of these dreams may have come and gone. To the women who have fulfilled their earlier dreams, we say, "Wonderful, well done! That's what life is all about; that's what we are here for!" In fact, we'd like to see you encourage other women to do the same and be a role model for them.

Dreams are not just for childhood. We'd guess the majority of you reading this book still have unfulfilled desires you've always set aside for what have appeared to be valid reasons. For example, "I don't have enough time," "not enough money," "I can't do that, my family won't approve," "I have more practical considerations right now."

There are more reasons than we care to mention that can get us women to stop ourselves from doing what we, and we alone, want and need for ourselves. It only makes sense that we would have this tendency because it's what we've been brought up to believe we should do. Unfortunately many of us were told the opposite of what would have helped us become all that we are capable of becoming. There are, of course, some who did receive full support. What about you? Just take a little time to think back to the messages you received as a child from your family, teachers, society, etc.—all of whom, of course, were trying to give you the very best advice they knew how. Were you given encouragement when sharing your ideas, thoughts, and dreams? Or did you hear something different? How often did you hear things like, "Oh, here you go dreaming again" or "Who do you think you are?" or "How do you expect to do that?" or "Well, honey, that might be OK for a boy, but not for a girl"?

Dreams and desires are neither frivolous nor too big to attempt; they are worthy of your time and attention. That's why we've asked you to list at least ten in an earlier exercise! Let's look at this logically. There is a reason you have these longings otherwise you wouldn't have them. Think about that…why would these yearnings present themselves to you unless there was a purpose? We firmly believe these yearnings come from the core of who you are and lead you to who you are meant to be on this earth. Now go back to the

"So, Who Am I?" exercise: What do your dreams or desires tell you about who you are at your core?

What is so important and what we are so passionate about is that you realize it is critical for you to do the thing you dream of, to follow through on your purpose here on earth. You will feel more satisfaction, joy, and fulfillment; and there is no doubt those around you will benefit too from these feelings. What is more, you will open the way for others to see what is possible for them. You can have a life richer than you've ever imagined...and the good news is it isn't too late; it's never too late. Actually, now is a perfect time!

So, armed with a greater awareness of who you are and being in touch with some of your current dreams, let us now explore more deeply by investigating some of the contexts in which you, along with many other women of "our age," may find yourself. As you read, we ask that you be curious and definitely apply no judgment to yourself. It's good to know your starting point, to get in touch with where you are. However, this book sees you as an individual—a unique person with your own unique set of circumstances, and it is with this individual that we shall work. So, the locating is for you—it's important and allows you to get the best out of the subsequent sections.

CHAPTER TWO

Midlife Crisis—
A View on Mortality

What exactly is this phenomenon we call "midlife crisis"? We see it is more of an issue for some women than for others, and the experience varies from person to person. Basically it is a stage of life when awareness of one's own mortality becomes highlighted. It is a time when one has thoughts such as: "Is this it?" "Where am I headed?" "What have I done with my life?" "How much time do I have left?" These sorts of questions create a feeling of "need to do more," of "time's running out fast," and can, if we let them, do nothing but raise our level of anxiety. Know that these are mere indicators that it is time to reevaluate your choices. Remember how we've already said it isn't too late. You have a choice, you can let time rush along and take you, or *you* can take the time you have and live it more fully. Midlife crisis is one reason the time is *now*!

First, you need to get a good sense of where you are missing out. Take a few moments and go deep within to do some reflecting on the choices you are making right now. Sit comfortably, close your eyes, breathe deeply into your body for a moment or two, and let your mind be quiet. Then see what answers arise to the following questions:

- *Where aren't you satisfied?*
- *What matters most to you?*
- *How much of your time is spent on what matters most?*
- *What's getting in the way of devoting time to what matters to you?*
- *If you knew you only had a year to live and you would be healthy and feeling well, what would you do with your time?*
- *What would add more "juice" to your life? Remember, age is just a number.*

Perhaps you have discovered that your past, even present accomplishments are no longer giving you the same level of satisfaction they once did; you've been there, done that, so to speak. You may be feeling an unsettling lack of direction. This is understandable since it is innate in humans to need a sense of direction, a sense of purpose. By going deep within and listening for the answers to these questions you can get in touch with your life purpose, what makes you tick. These are not answers that are in your head but rather at the core of your being. Listening requires sorting out the "should do's" from the "want to's." Who are you, what is it that makes you tick? Your life purpose will not be found in the "shoulds"; it resides within the "wants," "desires," and "dreams."

If you are in a midlife crisis state and feeling pressure, let's give you a little challenge. Notice when you say "I have to…" or "I should.…" How true are these statements? Are you making a conscious choice, clearly aware of the possible outcomes of your choice? Or are you just letting your subconscious run the show and following old unquestioned beliefs and patterns that were planted in your mind?

- *Examine your beliefs and patterns. Which ones were you taught by your family, teachers, society, etc.?*

- *Take a closer look at those beliefs and ask if they are really true for you.*
- *What do you truly believe?*
- *Review the patterns you follow on a daily basis. How necessary are they?*
- *What choices do you have and what might be the consequences?*

Let's use as an example any simple task, like making your bed each morning. Why do we do it? First, it may be founded on a belief that "you don't leave a bed unmade." Next, it is probably part of your morning pattern or routine. Now ask yourself, is it absolutely necessary? What is the reason to make the bed? Does it bring you satisfaction or pleasure? Do you like seeing the bed made and enjoy getting into an orderly bed at night? Or, is it simply a "should" …something you believe you are supposed to do? Or maybe a pattern you have gotten into?

Now, we are not saying you need to stop making your bed; nor are we saying you must stop doing other things you normally do. What we are asking you to do is to be mindful and check in with those "musts" and "shoulds." Find out where you spend your time and energy, then reevaluate to see if it is something you believe in and if it brings value to you.

We used to live with a list as long as your arm of all the things we *had* to do; it was just a part of living a normal day-to-day existence. Many of the things we are taught to believe (the "shoulds") vary from culture to culture, family to family, and religion to religion. The key is to uncover deep down inside what *you* believe, what has meaning for *you*…and what doesn't. So often we unwittingly collude with made-up stories about what we should do, and so they get perpetuated.

Lynn:

One of the things we were asked to do during our coach training was to list all the things we "have to" do. You might want to do that right now. If you look carefully at your list you will be able to see that none of them *has* to be done. For instance, you don't *have* to clean the house *every* Saturday; you don't even *have* to work for a living. Yes, of course, there are consequences to not doing so but you are fooling yourself if you genuinely think it *must* be done. This is how we get caught in all sorts of traps.

When I did this exercise during training, one of the many things I wrote down was "I have to be in paid employment" (even though I had a long-standing dream of working for myself). It was something of a revelation to me for someone to say, "No you don't," and I resisted it long and hard for a while. Then I reflected on what they had said. Indeed there would be consequences but I didn't in fact *have* to be in paid employment. They had said, "You can choose paid employment if you wish…and you need to know why you are choosing it. What are the benefits you want to have as a result of choosing to stay in paid employment?"

Once I had reflected on this it gave me two key pointers: 1) As long as I knew I was choosing to be in paid employment, I had a much better attitude toward it, with far less resentment, and 2) I knew I could choose to change the situation once I became aware of the possible consequences and which of them I was prepared to accept. I was able to design the life I wanted.

After a couple of years this enabled me to start my own business. The consequences were moving to a smaller house for a while so that there was no mortgage, something I was prepared to accept for my husband's peace of mind.

*As you swim around in the zone we call "midlife crisis,"
you are likely to find yourself feeling disappointed that
you did not have time for something you wanted or that life
didn't develop as you would have liked.*

- *What's a disappointment you've been carrying with you?*
- *What disappointment are you willing to let go of?*

When we are able to let go of negative emotions, such as feelings of disappointment, it gives us space for so much more to happen in our lives. It is one thing to allow ourselves to feel disappointment, sadness, anger, resentment; yet it is another thing to hang on to them. Yes, we must thoroughly feel our emotions, not deny them. Yet holding on to them won't allow you the space to move forward; holding on weighs you down and restricts you in many ways. In any case, if these disappointments are in the past, there's no going back to recoup them, and thinking about them only saps your energy.

In our workshops we talk with participants about the "loads" they are carrying around with them—the "if onlys," the disappointments in life, the negative emotions of anger, hatred, annoyance, or resentment. Then we get participants to "own" these loads by dancing with potatoes held between their knees, under their chin, and/or in other obscure places. The potatoes represent the weights, the "baggage" they carry with them through life. We choose these awkward ways of carrying because, in reality, we do not carry our own "baggage" in an evenly distributed way. The participants notice how much they are hindered in their dancing, making it impossible for them to move freely in a way that they would like.

Ahhh, the freedom, when they are prepared to commit to letting go of the negative emotion or thought epitomized by dropping the potatoes! Suddenly they are so much freer, looser, more able to take on and flow with the rhythm of the music.

It is the same in real life. You aren't physically carrying potatoes between your knees or under your chin; however, you are weighted down with stress and strain from negative emotions and thoughts you are holding onto. You will feel the same freedom the women in our workshops feel when you drop a negative emotion, when you choose an empowering perspective or way of looking at things. And this is the crux: You can choose how you want to see an issue—negatively or positively. The choice is yours. By choosing the positive, you become lighter, and possibilities become more clear and available to you.

- *What "weights" do you carry around with you that stop or limit you?*
- *What new way can you find to look only positively at these issues?*
- *What new choices can you make with the space that opens up for you?*

We have a friend Linda who decided that she was going to fulfill the ambition of a lifetime—she was going to live in Paris. This meant a major "letting go," along with making some huge changes that included selling the house that was her dream home, creating a totally new and very different relationship with her husband (they would live apart for much of the time), moving the essentials of her old home into her former family home. Linda then packed a bag and left to find a place in Paris. She had no knowledge of French and no contacts. The pull of finding this new life in a city that expressed her soul was so great that she now spends three or four months a year there.

What is interesting is that she had felt this pull for many, many years and was held back by her own sack of potatoes: her business, her dream house, her relationship.

> Once she let go of them, Linda was able to design something that worked, and with it came a realization that her "dream" home was a millstone preventing her from fulfilling her dreams and so it had to go.

In the movie *Calendar Girls*, what inspired a group of older women to take off their clothes to pose for calendar photos? Was it just a bit of fun, or something else? The movie has inspired lots of others to do something that they previously considered too bold or viewed as a "cannot" or "should not." We know of a group of women who took off their clothes for a "Goddesses as Leaders" calendar—all of them are over fifty. They not only dropped their clothes, they dropped a multitude of heavy emotions…those weights that would tell them they were too old or their bodies were not good enough, etc.

Right about now you may be raising your eyebrows and thinking, "What? Are they trying to persuade me to pose nude?" And, of course, we are not—unless it happens to be something you yearn to do!

What we are saying is midlife crisis happens, and we can view it as an awakening, an opportunity to ramp up the volume and claim the life that is ours even more.

CHAPTER THREE

Empty Nester—Where Have All My Interests Gone?

Are you an "empty nester"? Oh, for some women this is a real challenge. The mothering and caregiving instinct has run the show for so long, it can feel like the rug has been pulled out from under you. It can be a time of feeling unneeded and unwanted. Many of us find ourselves looking for things we can *do* to help our adult children, and sometimes this is an unconscious attempt to try to hold onto them. The effect can actually be that we hold our children back, not allowing them to grow and become as independent as they could be. It certainly doesn't allow a healthy adult-to-adult relationship to develop, *and* at the same time we hold ourselves back from moving on to the next stage of our life, from discovering what is possible and what may be waiting for us. It certainly isn't uncommon to feel a sense of emptiness when the house is quiet. Yet we can view this as an opening to those new activities that we've been putting off.

So, although we are missing our family, it is a perfect time to take advantage of the space we have to explore new outside interests. What else sparks your attention? What about prioritizing you and your needs that may have been set aside for years? Remember that list you made earlier? Doing this can be confusing since it is so new, and therefore it is very important to be gentle with yourself as you explore. It doesn't mean you aren't going to want to spend time with your children. It doesn't mean you are no longer a "good mother," that you no longer care. It means it is a new time for you when both you and those around you will benefit if you look forward. Do grieve the loss that you feel; it is important to your emotional and physical well-being to acknowledge and be with your feelings. However, it is equally important not to get stuck and dwell in them.

There are many ways of approaching this new phase of your life with a positive attitude, an attitude of renewal. Once the family has moved out, you have the freedom to recreate what your life will look like; you can reinvent your day-to-day lifestyle. This might be the first opportunity you have had to pursue new interests and consider your needs and desires, to give to *yourself* the time and energy you previously gave to the family's needs. What better time than now to resurrect and reevaluate the dreams and desires you had put aside for the family? It is up to you to determine how you want to spend your free time now that family responsibilities have diminished. Check out some of your habits—the time you get up, the time you feel you have to be home after you have been out shopping or following one of your interests. There are even big habits to be monitored—how much grocery shopping to do now that the children have left home, for example.

Notice if you feel guilty or selfish when contemplating an activity that would be fulfilling for you and does not involve the family. What does the small voice inside tell you that you want? What other messages are coming through? Are they negative, like "that would be selfish" or "I can't sit and read in the middle of the afternoon…I've got to accomplish something…"? Some positive messages to replace the negative are: "This is self-care and self-love" and "I can only give love to others if I first love and give to myself." Get the picture? These are true *statements.*

We'll continue to say this: We cannot give to another what we haven't given to ourselves first; it's not possible because it isn't there to give. If this is not something you truly believe, please spend time reflecting on it. It is one of the biggest obstacles, particularly for us women. We are generally givers, and yet if our cup isn't full, we can't fill the cup of another. Are you a giver? Do you give and give and then wonder why you feel depleted? It is at these times of total depletion that other feelings such as resentment, even anger, can creep in. Perhaps you feel satisfied in the giving but something is not quite right. You aren't feeling truly fulfilled; something is missing. Does this resonate with you…a great deal or even a little?

Let's now take a closer look at your relationship with your children. Society has always put an emphasis on the role of "mother," to such an extent that the expectations of a mother are too high for any normal human to meet. And guess what, we mothers tend to feel we must meet these expectations even if they are unrealistic. It is for that reason some women believe they must be superior to their children simply because they are the mother. We know of women who hold this belief. In their minds, if they are not wiser and smarter than their children it means they aren't a good mother and in general not good enough. Their self-esteem is highly affected by their relationship with their children.

Take a moment to consider your view of yourself as a mother. It may be something you have not reflected on before, so take your time, give it your attention.

To help you gain clarity, you may want to reflect a little on your behaviors and the beliefs that lie beneath them with regard to your role as mother. Some of these questions may seem harsh and yet many times our motives are unconscious and unclear to us. What mother doesn't want to be special in the eyes of her children? All of us want that. Yet sometimes the way in which we go about getting that special feeling isn't always healthy for us, or our children.

- *Do you notice if you are always trying to "fix" your children or events that occur in their lives?*
- *Do you believe your children love you and want to spend time with you for what you can do for them rather than simply because of who you are?*
- *If your children handle things perfectly fine without you, do you believe you aren't loved or you aren't valued and admired?*
- *Do you feel some sense of self-worth if your children can't handle things on their own as well as when you are helping or involved?*
- *Are you afraid that if your children do become totally independent, you will lose them or won't see them?*
- *If they surpass you in their abilities, what does that say about you?*

Whatever your answers to these questions, some of you will be very pleased, and some of you may be surprised and perhaps not too pleased. The important point is to become aware of your beliefs, motives, and behaviors, so it is crucial that you answered the questions honestly and authentically from where you are now without judging yourself.

As a mother you don't want to get stuck equating your value as a mother or as a person with how much you can do for your children. The fact that you are their mother and have raised them through good and bad times to the best of your ability is what matters. In the here and now, "who" you are being…how you show up as a person, how much you show respect, empathy, and support for your children is what defines your worth as a mother. So many new perspectives can be explored. Letting go will allow your children to grow and thrive as they become more self-sufficient, and their respect, love, and admiration for you will increase as they experience this newfound independence and discovery of themselves. As this occurs, a new relationship can be established—adult-to-adult—with just as much love and possibly more respect than ever before. As a mother one can take great pride when children don't "need" mother, yet "want" mother, because that is what true love is. Needing does not compare to wanting when it comes to love; wanting is a conscious choice whereas needing is a dependence.

Let's take a look at the concept of letting go from a different perspective that can be lots of fun. We are talking about letting go of material items to create the new physical environment that will better match the new lifestyle you are creating. It can be a matter of de-cluttering, or perhaps a larger change like downsizing and living more simply. Let's start with something that is easier to do. What material items, clothes, etc., have been gathering dust in your closet, attic, or basement? Do you want them or need them? Be selective. What is worth keeping? What is just creating more clutter in your world? Remember, what clutters our physical environment also clutters our mind and emotions. And what about your home? Is it too large for you now, or do you enjoy and still love the space you are living in?

We aren't saying that everyone needs to de-clutter and downsize; this is an individual choice and differs from person to person. At the same time it is more than likely that you, and most of us, have accumulated belongings in various corners of your home that you may not even remember you have. Take stock of this to see what is best for you; what will lighten your load and give you more space both physically and metaphorically?

If you are married or in a long-term relationship, this is the ideal time to revitalize your relationship. You can renew and redesign it by beginning to get to know one another better and doing some deep listening. With the responsibilities of raising children our relationships with our husbands or partners can suffer without our noticing it. Time passes and we do not realize all the changes that occur through the years. Both of you will have grown and changed as partners and as individuals. Now is the time to get to know one another at a deeper level, a time to deepen the connection. Yes, despite the years and the familiarity, there is always more to explore and learn about each other.

Julie:

At the time our children were all moving out, my husband and I noticed that our lives felt a bit empty. We have three children and were accustomed to the activities that involved the children, even just watching a movie together or having a conversation. We wanted to recharge our relationship and wondered how we'd be able to do it since we both were in high-demand careers; we were like passing ships in the night. We decided we could begin to make "dates" with one another. We committed to sitting down together every Saturday morning to review our individual schedules and pick at least two times during the week when we would schedule an activity or just plan time to spend together. This time was carved out on each of our calendars and we agreed that if something came up that prevented us from having the date at the prearranged day and time, we would immediately reschedule within the same week.

What we learned is that most weeks, although we only scheduled two dates, more spots opened up and we were able to spend an even greater amount of time together. We then looked at some outside activities we had talked about in the past. One of those was dancing, so we took dance lessons and began going out dancing more often, just the two of us. It has turned out to be very romantic, rejuvenating, and great fun.

- *How much alone time have the two of you been able to spend over the years with the children at home?*

- *What activities have the two of you not been able to participate in together that you would like to?*

CHAPTER FOUR

Sandwich Generation— Merely the Filling?

What about the "sandwich generation"? We hear this term so much, and when you are in it, it can be a huge challenge. Many women feel as if they are caught in a trap, a trap where there appears to be no option to take care of themselves. It is a time of high demand, sandwiched between the children who are probably young adults eager to find their feet and their voice, and the older generation who are requiring duty to be paid. The younger generation may still be living at home and needing attention. In some cases they may still be very young children not even in their teens. The older generation (parents and in-laws) are requiring assistance and/ or caregiving; perhaps they are no longer able to drive, handle their own business affairs, or worse, physically or mentally restricted. This is an increasingly common phenomenon, with women having children later and parents living longer and benefiting from the improvements in healthcare and medication.

So here we are…our child-raising days aren't finished so we still have a great deal of responsibility with our children's lives, and then responsibilities increase even more due to the needs of the elderly in the family.

If you fit in this category, how are you handling it? You may believe you only have one option: to take care of everyone and set your needs aside. You continue to fill the needs of your immediate family in your home and you jump in and do what is needed for the elderly. Meanwhile, there is nothing left for you. Your love, compassion, and commitment are admirable and at the same time, if you aren't taking time for your own needs, you are selling out on yourself and aren't at your best with your family. You may think you would be selfish to choose any other way, that anything you do for yourself will only detract from what you can do for the other two generations in your life. You allow yourself to feel guilty and responsible if they aren't getting everything from you.

Lynn:

My version of being a part of the sandwich generation was that I had overstayed my development in a job believing that I couldn't move because of my husband's business and my daughter's schooling—plus a pull from my parents that if I moved again I would have to move nearer to where they lived.

Eventually, when I was forty-eight, I realized that I didn't know who I was anymore other than someone who felt like she was being batted around from one crisis to another—crisis management at work; crisis helping with the business; crisis being a bad parent to my daughter; crisis not doing my duty for my parents. I felt like I was drowning.

It was then that I determined it was time for me to do something about myself. I had refused to go to a university when I was younger and although I had good qualifications, I had never gotten a degree. So I decided to go whole hog and work toward an MBA while still working full-time in a very demanding job. In doing this there were a number of things I had to give up and say no to, including close national involvement in my special rare breed of dogs (though I didn't get rid of the dogs!).

At the time I was quite proud of the way I handled it— discussing my desires with my husband and daughter, getting their commitment at least to understand that this was something I wanted to do for me, and the impact it was likely to have on them. Three years later I made it, even through the traumas of having to stay up all night to finish assignments and then go into work the next day and of losing my job and starting a new job. I learned many a lesson on the way and while I didn't realize it for a couple of years, doing a module on Creative Management introduced me to many aspects that are akin to coaching. So it even served to illuminate my next path!

It was one of my proudest moments when I wore a master's cap and gown on my graduation day. This experience allowed me to let go of gremlins about my past and gave me a sense of my own identity that has continued to grow.

On the other hand, you could be taking totally the opposite approach—avoidance. You may be trying to escape from it all. Indeed it may not even be very clear to you that you are taking "avoiding" action because it can take on different forms, such as a new career, especially a very demanding one; spending more time at your job; more schooling; etc.

Let's be clear that this is not about judging what you in your unique circumstances should be doing. We are pointing to the need to take a clear view on your own actions. Starting a new career does not automatically mean you are trying to escape being the filling in the sandwich. Sometimes however there is a hidden agenda beneath the surface of our behavior. It is possible to fool ourselves into thinking we "must" do something when in fact we are not making a conscious choice.

Julie:

One day I found myself in a very fast-paced job and lifestyle and wondered how I had gotten there. It wasn't how I wanted to be living my life. From there it didn't take too long to figure out I had been escaping. Yes, escaping from the chaos in my home, from my three growing children and a husband who, from my perspective, were all doing what they wanted. There didn't seem to be room for what I wanted, and I even lost track of *what* I wanted. I had elderly parents and in-laws who began needing so much and expecting so much…there was no room for me to have my own life and my own space to do what I needed. Others all wanted something different from me. Or, at least so it seemed to me.

On some level I must have been thinking that diving into the responsibilities of my career would allow me to avoid totally losing myself. How could I lose myself when for the first time in my life I would be creating an identity that was independent of my family? Of course, the real me could surface and I would flourish. Well, I learned differently; I unconsciously continued with old habits of putting others first and did lose myself and what I truly needed anyway.

I focused on fulfilling the expectations of my customers and the corporation I worked for without taking what I needed into much consideration. In essence, I was repeating what I had done at home: trying to be so good at everything and accomplishing so much while I suffered inside. After experiencing a confusing mixture of satisfaction, disappointment, and discomfort, I finally came to realize that my codependency—my need to give to others and to receive approval—is what I needed to understand and change; otherwise I would continue to lose myself no matter what the circumstances. *I*, not necessarily my environment, needed to change.

This is where I learned firsthand that we cannot fill the cup of another—the concept we've mentioned before—whether it is family, customers, or indeed anyone else, if we are not filling our own cup. Once I learned to give to myself, I became more satisfied, more energized, more at peace. And it hasn't been a quick and easy lesson for me; I am still learning to give to myself! Remember the saying, "Life is a journey not a destination"? Well, as long as the journey continues I want to keep exploring and learning…that's what the journey is all about!

Take a look at what you are doing and reflect on the reason and its meaning for you. It is important for you to make a conscious choice—whatever that might be—that is about you and your life. If you discover you are not choosing, just reacting, then it would do you well to take a closer look.

To help you gain clarity on this closer look, ask yourself the questions below. You may add other questions of your own too.

- *How is your new career, longer working hours, going to school—or whatever you have chosen—bringing you fulfillment?*
- *How well-suited is it for who you really are? Is there something missing? Perhaps the career or the classes aren't satisfying?*
- *How energizing and engaging are those extra hours you are dedicating to working or studying?*

If you're experiencing doubt, could it be that keeping busy is making you less available to what feels like overwhelming family responsibilities?

As you reflect you may realize there has been a positive outcome to what may have started out as an escape. Perhaps the state of your life was the original impetus to moving forward in a good direction for you. Initially you decided on something to escape, and while doing so found what brings you joy and value now and in the future. Take a long look, what do you see? What do you hear your inner voice telling you?

There is another escape that is definitely an unconscious one. Being able to see nothing but the "must do" for others can result in your becoming ill, and at that point you must make a choice. You can choose to put yourself into the equation when looking at everyone else's needs and start some self-care, or you can choose to continue in the old way and take the chance that you may become seriously ill. Illness is an alarm call, one way the universe gets your attention. You are the only one who can make the choice. Self-care most definitely includes being gentle and compassionate with yourself. You count as much as the next person…you are equal.

So what healthy options are there? For one, there is what we said earlier: Put yourself and your needs and desires into the equation. Look at the bigger picture. Let's face it, when you put your needs aside, you can't possibly be showing up at your fullest potential as a mom or a daughter or a daughter-in-law. Ideally you want to give love and assistance unconditionally and from your heart, but when you are running on empty yourself how is that possible? You risk burnout.

There are also options that are not immediately visible. Ask yourself, "What other way is there?" Perhaps asking for help from other family members or friends can alleviate some of your burden. How about exploring what the family, whether the younger generation or the older, can actually do for themselves? How much help do they really need? This is where old beliefs need to be reevaluated. Is it true you are the only one who can take care of your mom "right," or the only one who "should" be doing it? Finding new ways to help doesn't mean you care any less; actually you care more since you are looking at the well-being of all concerned.

There are of course instances when there aren't too many viable options. An example is if you (or your husband) are an only child and your parents (or his) live a very long distance from you. It is possible there isn't anyone else you can rely on, which leaves you little choice but to handle the affairs yourself. Even so, there are always new ways of looking at the situation—we strongly encourage you to open your mind to any and all possibilities. Take everything into consideration that could reduce your load no matter how insignificant it may seem. Take time for yourself whenever you can. In the long run, if you are able to eliminate some of the smaller duties and have some time to yourself, you will reduce your stress.

Lynn:

Sadly my mother and I never got on very well. My own personal growth journey started too late for me to be able to use it to truly understand what the issue was. Nevertheless, I wanted the best care for her when she started to show early signs of dementia and could no longer carry on the independent life she loved in safety.

Where I come from, one's duty is to look after aging parents. My mother left no doubt that is what I should be doing. Yet it was very clear to me there was no way I could have my mother live with me. Through family arguments and difficulties she had already pushed her only granddaughter and her son-in-law away. This left just me to sort things out directly with my mother. So the situation was that while I received support from my family, I got no direct assistance in the care of my mother.

I insisted on finding residential care near to where I lived to make things viable for me. I needed to handle this well enough so that my mother was as happy as she could be and I could keep most of my life intact.

It was clear to me right from the start how much residential care helped to spread the load and at the same time provided my mother with the sorts of diversions that filled her day in an enjoyable way. In other words, it provided care and support that I alone could not provide. It also helped me keep the quality time I spent with her in perspective, since I knew that any other way would have skewed my life totally and I was not prepared to make this choice. The choice I did make was done consciously, free from any sense of guilt.

I know it is not the path that others would choose and I value their choices too. What was special for me was that I was able to make the choice and design a way that was a win-win for everyone as far as possible.

There is a fine line we cross between serving and fixing someone. When doing for someone, how much of it could they do for themselves? Are you serving them or are you trying to fix them? There is a difference. When serving, we are actually supporting someone to do for themselves. In that way the other person feels respected and can maintain some sense of dignity and independence, even better health and self-esteem in the long run. Helping them be their best may mean doing some things for them, but not everything.

> *To serve is beautiful, but only if it is done with joy and a whole heart and a free mind.*
>
> —Pearl S. Buck

There is a story about Liz and the responsibility she continued to feel toward her daughter through the years. Liz left her husband, and as a result her daughter, then a young teenager, had to sell her horse.

After more than twelve years Liz still felt guilty and therefore had difficulty saying no to her daughter. She helped her build her life financially, with huge donations of time and a lot of expenditure of emotional energy. The day I asked her, "How long is the sentence you have imposed on yourself?" was the day the light bulb went on. She had no idea she was still punishing herself by constantly fixing things for her daughter. She saw that it was neither serving her, nor her daughter. Letting go of her guilt was one of the biggest shifts she has had in her life—and it was nothing other than letting go of self-limiting thoughts about a past that is no longer real. Her thoughts were keeping it alive…her daughter in particular had no idea that this was behind her mother's hugely intrusive support.

Working in a way that serves her daughter—listening and not advising, acknowledging and championing, allowing for her daughter's wisdom to come through—has made a huge difference to Liz. It has changed her relationship with her daughter into something that is much more akin to deep friendship and has given her loads of space that is no longer taken up by all the guilty thoughts.

Love can smother. When we begin to do too much for others, their own ability to do for themselves diminishes; they believe they can no longer do small tasks they were once able to do or, in the case of the young ones, they never get the opportunity to learn from trying and failing. They become accustomed to someone else doing it. They begin to believe they aren't capable and do not develop self-esteem and confidence.

Stop reading and go within…ponder at a deep level these questions:

- *Think of something someone does for you on a regular basis that perhaps you are capable of doing yourself. How does it feel? What will happen if the other person is not there for you someday? Does this prospect cause you any disquiet? As time goes by do you start to feel inadequate?*

- *Now, think of when someone supports you…how does it feel being supported to do for yourself? How much more empowered do you feel?*

- *What is your belief about how much you are responsible for family members? How much support do you "want" to give them versus how much do you believe you "should" give them?*

Truth is, we all feel much better about ourselves when we maintain as much independence as possible. The true gift you can give to your family is real heartfelt support.

When you develop a habit of taking time for things that bring you joy, spending free time, be it going to the park, indulging in a pamper session, or simply sitting and reading, you become less stressed, more joyful, and in general maintain a better mood. You are not the only one to benefit—your family and those around you do too! Isn't your giving nature more authentic when you are in a better space yourself? What are you doing just for yourself, regardless of whether the family agrees with or is also interested in it?

Think of how hindered you are in giving unconditionally when you are running on empty. What are your ways of filling and replenishing your personal energy tank? We'll work with you more on this in Section Two.

Although we do not have a choice about being a member of the sandwich generation, we do have a choice as to how we see ourselves as the filling. The truth is there is no need to spread ourselves too thin. So, to continue with the metaphor, there is no sandwich without a filling—and for the filling to be good, it needs to be rich and plentiful. For it to be rich and plentiful, it needs loving care.

CHAPTER FIVE

Retirement and Impending Retirement—With a Flourish

Sooner or later I'm going to die, but I'm not going to retire.

—Margaret Mead

The prospect or reality of retirement may be rearing its head. When retirement is impending, the anticipation that it will be great to be free from the daily grind can be so exhilarating that you do not think of anything else. You are filled with wonderful thoughts of sleeping until you are ready to get up instead of when the alarm clock rings…of not having to sit in rush-hour traffic…oh, the freedom you will have! Initially that freedom can have you feeling like you are floating on air and yet as time passes, as with anything else, things change and you find yourself coming back down to earth with a thud. In truth when you retire if you haven't a solid idea of how you want to spend your free time or what would satisfy you on a daily basis, retirement can leave you floundering. As a species we are not made to be directionless. Regardless of age, everyone needs their own sense of purpose.

Then again, you may have listened to your intuition and had the foresight to prepare yourself for retirement—laying the foundation for a new career by investigating your options, taking classes, collaborating with others, etc. Or maybe you have plenty of interests and hobbies that will keep you absorbed and feeling alive. If this is the case, we salute you for taking charge, designing your lifestyle, and seeing the potential in this phase of your life.

We have a friend who has done just that.

When Theresa was in her early thirties she was drawn to energy work and took a class in self-healing. At that time she was a full-time wife and mother raising a family of five children. After taking the class, she had an experience that validated her interest and abilities in this area; however, as so often happens, life got in the way—after all, she had a household to manage and a husband and five children to attend to! So she let the energy work drop away.

In her late forties Theresa was drawn to enter the university to earn a master's in social work, and with that degree she went out into the world as a social worker at the age of fifty—something was missing though, but what?

As Theresa was approaching sixty-three years of age and was looking forward to retiring in two years, she had no idea what she would do in retirement. Being very spiritual she always delved into areas that called to her. It was at this time that the energy healing work reappeared in her life seemingly out of nowhere. Based on someone's suggestion, she read a couple of books about energy healing, and as she read, her excitement rose. Energy healing resonated so very deeply with her even after all those years had passed.

Theresa read whatever she could, practiced some, and knew deep in her heart that she had to follow through with it this time—no letting it go again. Because she was no longer married and was supporting herself, it would have been easy for Theresa to let old logic and financial fears sway her, but she didn't. She found a way to make it work: She managed her finances and used her vacation time to attend shaman training with one of the most prestigious organizations. As she was in the learning stage, she offered her services for free. Now that she has completed her training and is retired, she has been able to build a fee-based practice as a modern-day shaman. As we write this she is just turning sixty-six and is more engaged and thriving than ever before in her life—all this while bringing a great service to other people.

So, what's your perspective on retirement? Is it one of exhilaration, or are you looking at retirement as a penalty, not welcoming the thought of being home all the time? Or, does the thought of having your husband or partner at home all day fill you with delight or dread?

Maybe you are curious, wondering what the two of you will do when you are both retired: "How will we spend our time?" "Will we get on each other's nerves?" "Will he start rearranging my spice rack if he's bored?" (We know of a woman whose husband did this in retirement.) Ugh, the many doubts can leave you feeling very stressed out! You can of course focus on having more time for vacation preparations, the vacations themselves, and various activities. However, there is an awful lot of time in between vacations and these other activities. How are you going to view that time and space? What will *you* want to do individually as well?

Some who are already retired may have experienced a loss of identity and purpose. We are sure that those of you who are preparing to retire need to be aware of this possibility. If your career and/or job has consumed most of your life, you may very likely feel a loss of identity when you leave it. Many of us strongly identify with our jobs and careers since they provide a mirror of our accomplishments and of the quantity and quality of our relationships with other people. When we retire, we leave those accomplishments behind and for the most part the relationships as well. We no longer have the mirror that we relied on so much. What will fill the void in terms of activities and relationships? How will you avoid isolation in retirement? What will keep you out in the world with people?

Having a hobby, artistic pursuits, or volunteering; connecting with family; traveling; being out in the world…whatever attracts you can pull you out of bed in the morning with pep in your step.

Uncovering what you are interested in will allow you to create a new identity…the real you. Remember, what you choose to fill your time with does not have to be what someone else does or considers valuable. It doesn't have to be according to society's—or indeed anyone else's—standards. It is vital to find out what it is for *you*.

Let's also take a look at friends. Earlier we spoke about how your circle of friends can change as you make changes in your life. After retirement it will be wise to make a point of maintaining friendships that you value and creating new ones too. You may think you will stay connected to former co-workers. However, unless you make the effort, the relationships can dwindle. After all, you won't be seeing them every day and you will have less in common. You will be amazed how quickly the daily gossip, the politics of the place appear to be less enticing, less interesting. That doesn't mean you must drop the friendship; if you enjoyed the company of another while working with her/him then there certainly is something beyond work that can be the basis of your friendship. Preserving and establishing your community of friends and associates will serve as a big support as you go through this transition.

We're highlighting community because once you are out of the workforce your world may seem smaller. Unless you have outside activities you will be engaged in on a regular basis or unless you have a firmly established community of friends and associates, you may feel isolated. This feeling of isolation can be very disturbing, particularly if you have been in a career where you interfaced with many people on a regular basis. Even if you have worked in a small company with few co-workers, you were accustomed to seeing others and talking and being with them daily. Once retired, that won't be the case, unless of course you live with a large family. Being in community can be of great value. Contact current acquaintances and friends whose company you enjoy and get out there and meet new people.

We know a woman, Lydia, who dreamed of the day she would retire, thinking that she would be free to do what she wanted, not what she had to do at work. She dreamed of the free time to do all the things she never had time for. Once she retired, the excitement wore off within a couple of months. She then found herself at loose ends, not knowing what she wanted. After a great deal of inner reflection she realized her job had given her a sense of purpose and pride, a reason for being. She also recognized she had a love of playfulness yet did not necessarily have a way of expressing it.

Aha, an insight for her; she connected the two and started a part-time job at a child care center. It gave her a sense of purpose and commitment that she was missing, provided her the arena to be playful and in community with others. Plus she still had free time to explore other interests and activities.

Since many of us retire at younger ages than previous generations, we have so many more years and so much to share with others. We can share ourselves by spending time with others or we can actually share what we know through teaching, or training, or writing, etc. Whatever you choose to do, be assured that you've got a great deal of experience and wisdom under your belt. How well you do in retirement is largely dependent on your self-perception and coming to grips with who you really want to be. When you come to terms with being yourself and with the state of "being" as opposed to identifying yourself with what you do and what you accomplish, we can guarantee the stress of life will reduce. You will be more flexible and able to flow with changes that occur. All in all you'll feel younger and others will love you for it.

As you move through this book you'll find that we refer quite a bit to "being." We often remind our clients that we are human beings, not human doings. Reflect for a moment on conversations, perhaps when you are talking with someone new. One of the first things you might ask, or be asked, is "What do you do?" How many times do you get asked the question, "Who are you?" So although much of what we've already said does imply that there is more for you to do, more for you to experience, there is the other consideration of learning to accept yourself for "who" you are and therefore being at peace with whatever you choose. And retirement is a great place for choices—there are many more choices than you may have had in the past; many more options than you've ever thought about. And we know that being faced with so many options can feel overwhelming at times.

Here is when the "shoulds" need to be weeded out, and this can be achieved by reflecting on what you want. You may want to simply "be" by sitting in the park, or in your backyard, watching the ocean, looking at the trees, or simply doing *nothing*. That is all wonderful. On the other hand, you may want to be "doing" some familiar things but from a less stereotypical perspective. For instance you may be choosing to spend more time babysitting your grandchildren so that you can *get to know them better*. Or you may want to spend more time with them *playing with childlike abandon and freedom yourself*. Now, wouldn't both grandmother and grandchildren benefit? And just look how having a different perspective can make the same activity seem very different.

> We have a wonderful example of someone who has mastered the art of retirement. Catherine is a friend who has retired no fewer than four times!
>
> The last time was on her seventieth birthday when she decided she wanted to spend more time traveling to see one of her daughters in Australia. Everyone was extremely surprised to hear her reason for retiring. No one could believe that she

had reached seventy—she is so vibrant, full of energy, and never, never complaining. In essence she does not see herself as anything other than healthy, vigorous, up-to-date, and with something special still to offer the many people she serves in her full life.

At fifty she left her husband for nearly two years before she came back into his life in a way that worked for her. They have been able to redesign and he has been able to accept that she is the strong, powerful partner in the partnership (something he could not live with earlier in their life)—and now he is happy to ferry her to different appointments and take on the cooking responsibilities when needed. They are very happy together and Catherine has her voice well and truly heard.

Keep in mind the above are simply examples to help you get thinking about the possibilities for yourself. They are not intended for you to start comparing yourself with others or thinking about yourself in a negative way. Instead, they are there to inspire you to explore your own potential and what may be possible for you. Here are some questions to help you ensure that your designed retirement is truly your own:

- *How do you perceive yourself in regard to retirement?*
- *What is retirement to you?*
- *What is your belief about making significant life changes at your age?*
- *What judgments do you hold that cause you to shape yourself to fit a certain image?*
- *What interests do you have?*
- *What might your interests translate into: something that has you sharing with others, getting out of the house?*
- *Who are the people you enjoy being with? What are their interests? Where are they?*

CHAPTER SIX

Fitness or Illness— Is There a Choice?

W e're bringing up a topic that may make you smile broadly or may cause you to groan, or maybe something in between. Your health. It goes without saying that at every stage of our lives our health, physical fitness, diet, and general well-being are crucial to us. How we experience life and what we are able to do or not do very much correlates with our health. Some of you will be thinking, "Hey, I'm doing just fine" and others may be thinking, "Hmmm, I guess I could use some improvement." Still others may be thinking, "I don't want to go there." We aren't going to continue listing the various reactions you could be having, of course, because there are too many possibilities here given that you are all unique individuals with your own set of circumstances.

This uniqueness is something to take into account when making choices that affect your health. Remember that you always have a choice in how you see your particular circumstances, and your choices *greatly* influence your health. Meanwhile, we are not implying that you have total *control* because that is not the case. Many factors play a role in our health: genetics, the environment, toxins, etc. So although you have a tremendous amount of power in making choices, we wouldn't want you to go overboard and blame yourself if you are or were to become ill. You do, however, always have a choice in how you deal with any illness that comes your way.

With that said, eating a balanced diet, exercising, and having a positive attitude contribute to our well-being, physically, mentally, and emotionally. However, what is best for one woman is not necessarily what is best for another. As individuals we need to educate ourselves and learn what is best for us. Yes, more self-discovery if you aren't already clear on what is best for you; that means learning how to listen for what *your* body needs and wants.

OK, get ready, because we've got more questions:

- *What is your belief around aging and health in general?*
- *How do you view your age and your health? Are you optimistic, do you never even think about it, or do you believe it is inevitable that you will go downhill as you age?*
- *How much influence do you believe you can have on your health and well-being?*
- *How do you view your body—physically, psychologically, emotionally?*
- *How aware are you of how different foods affect you? For instance, do you feel sluggish after eating certain foods? Do you feel more energetic after eating other types of food?*
- *And what about exercise?*
  - *Is the amount you get right for you and your body?*
  - *Is the type of exercise something you enjoy or dread?*
  - *Is the time of day you exercise right for you?*
  - *Do you exercise when you feel good or bad about yourself?*
- *What do you expect of your daily regime?*

Doing the best to maintain good health and fitness gives us more energy and a sense of aliveness. It will also help to eliminate any sense of guilt that some of us may be carrying when we aren't taking good care of ourselves. Eliminating guilt in and of itself contributes hugely to better health…think about it!

Now we'd like you to think a little more deeply about the statement "taking care of myself" because it's often not a phrase women use in a totally selfless way.

- *What does "taking care of myself" look like for you?*
- *What feelings come up when you think "take care of myself"?*

Have you made a habit of taking care of yourself or are you clueless? If you don't have a clue, then it is something you *must* learn; you owe it to yourself and to your health. You might be saying, "If I don't have a clue, how am I going to learn?" The answer to that is by paying close attention on a daily basis to your body and how it is feeling. At various times of the day, stop and feel the sensations in your body. What's going on in your stomach, your abdomen, your head, shoulders, back? Check out your entire body and if you notice discomfort or pain, see what adjustment you can make. Are you in a stressful situation, are you hungry, did you eat and now have some aftereffects? Stay in a place of pure curiosity as you scan your body. It won't take long, only a few minutes, and you will gradually learn more and more how to listen to your body in the moment. This listening in the moment will help you be on the alert for anything that needs your attention.

While on this topic, we can't go into denial and ignore the chance that many of us either are, will be, or have been challenged with a serious illness or accident. Realistically as we progress through the journey of life, we cannot totally avoid it all. It is a part of life and yet we are not usually taught how to deal with it, either in preparation or after the fact.

Typically, when an illness or injury pops into our lives, we simply aren't prepared for what it all means or what it will entail, how it may change our lives, how we may need to change our lifestyle and our perspectives on life. So when all this comes at once it feels like an even stronger body blow. Not only must we deal with the illness or injury, we must also undertake a good deal of soul searching so that it is possible to move into a perspective that will serve us.

If you are ill or if you are not in the shape you would like to be in, what changes do you need to make in the realm of self-care? What perspective about how you are needs to shift? What habits, if any, do you have that are contributing to the illness or your being out of shape?

A very powerful example of taking charge of one's own self-care is Maria, a woman of fifty-plus years who chose a new perspective when faced with a major challenge. She had undergone a mastectomy followed by chemotherapy and chose to approach her condition with resilience and wisdom. Living in a hot climate, she decided to be totally bald rather than wear a wig, scarf, or hat and she looked absolutely radiant!

Maria had found a way of living with the illness that was not going to get her down; her resilience shone through. Now she has secondary areas of cancer on her spine and yet she is so full of grace as she lives with the prospect of not knowing how long she is going to be around. She is working on her treatment with her oncologist, listening to her body, and understanding the stresses of medication that her body can or cannot take. She has become grateful for the small things in life and takes time to admire the beauty of nature around her. Her last set of tests showed nothing had changed over the past six months—there had been no deterioration.

Maria could have chosen to be resentful and bitter that not only did she have to undergo one experience of cancer but also is now being challenged a second time around. Yet she knows that *how* she chooses to live determines the quality of her life no matter how short or how long it may be.

All this is not to deny the feelings of sadness, anger, despair, and other emotions you must go through if a serious illness or injury causes any kind of limitation or restriction in your lifestyle. You have a right to feel all those emotions and it is important that you allow yourself to fully be with them and not fight them or try to push them down. Doing that only deepens and worsens the wounds. Surrendering to the emotion helps it to be processed in your body and lets it pass, as indeed everything does. It may feel that this will never happen. It pays to remember that even when we are experiencing great elation and fun, it doesn't last forever…the negative emotions don't either, especially when we fully allow ourselves to sit with them and know that they are a direct function of the quality of our thinking.

One way of looking at an illness is to view it as a wake-up call. It is telling us there's something we haven't seen or fully recognized. This doesn't mean that you caused the illness or injury. If you are facing illness or injury, what we are asking you to consider is that old choices, old ways of being may very well need some adjusting. What could have contributed to the illness? Eating too many unhealthy foods, having a pessimistic viewpoint, attempting to control everything, doing too much, being inflexible, or being too accommodating to everyone but yourself?

This is a perfect time to do some quiet reflection to uncover what can be extracted that is positive from this otherwise negative dilemma you find yourself in. What changes can you make? What about a new outlook on life in general, seeing more clearly what life is really about for you? Is it about being able to do what you have always done in the past? Think about this one…the healthy answer is no. A healthy approach is when we concentrate on the progress we can, and are, making from this point forward.

Julie:

I speak from my own personal experience when I say that if we open our minds to the different ways our life can look, we will fare much better, be healthier, live longer, and have more peace and joy.

When I was ill and had to have major surgery at the age of fifty-eight, I thought I would bounce back within two or three months as I had done with previous illnesses and surgeries. This time was different, however. I did *not* bounce back. I did anything but! Other health conditions that were probably present for some time became problems and obstacles in my life. My physical body and emotional body needed a well-deserved rest and recuperation period that was *much* longer than I had ever imagined. I, of course, became angry, frightened, and sad about the limitations I was forced to deal with. Not able to jump back into all the activities I was previously engaged in caused me to grieve a great deal. And the grieving was, of course, a critical piece of what I needed to do.

It took me months of reflection to realize I had been living such a fast-paced life that it was anything but balanced and fulfilling. That was a big one for me to fully admit since it caused me to wonder "How could that be? I'm a life coach, for heaven's sake." I was all about coaching others to honor their values and put balance back into their lives. Whoa, and here I was not even close to doing it for myself, although I *thought* I was!

What became so clear to me is that even though I was pursuing many passions with excitement and fun (believing I was following guidance from God) I was running on empty and trying to force things to happen in *my* time frame. During the lengthy recovery, I noticed when I stopped wishing things were different, stopped fretting about when I was going to be able to get moving again and just accepted how things were, and allowed myself to *be* and *feel* what I was feeling (even if it wasn't of my choosing) that my life flowed more smoothly. I immediately had less anxiety.

Previously I would ask myself many times on a daily basis, "What is the appropriate amount of accomplishment or activity for one day?" That question alone is an indicator of how much I previously had packed into a day and didn't have a clue what "flow" was…even though I talked about it all the time. In reality I had no idea. Intellectually I did, but not as a regular experience. I was driven by a belief that first I had to get things done, do something of value before I could just "be." Whereas the opposite is actually what I needed.

Another question I began asking myself is, "What does my ego want versus what does my soul want?" These activities I was pursuing, were they what I was meant to be doing…were they stepping stones?

You may want to ask yourself these same questions. Asking yourself questions is a way of seeking a deeper meaning and uncovering what is most important, what matters most.

Certainly we all want to be able to continue pursuing and doing all that we've done in the past. Yet if an illness or injury is preventing that, having a different viewpoint can be of great service to us. We can still feel young and fully alive inside by being different and doing different things. The positive energy that you have placed in certain areas prior to your illness can be directed in another area. As an example: Let's say you love the game of tennis and have played it well. Now you are no longer able to play tennis as well or perhaps you may not be able to play at all. That can be devastating to you. Grieve that loss, and then in the right time, move on. Remaining stuck and dwelling on what is no longer possible is destructive and will diminish the quality of your life. Look for another way to expend your energy. You might be good at teaching tennis to young people or the older generation. Then again it may be that tennis took up time that prevented you from exploring some other form of self-expression…maybe art.

The key message here is the sooner we can let go of resentment, of sadness, and other negative emotions, the sooner we can reduce the stress we are creating in ourselves and move on to something different.

> *Life appears to me to be too short to be spent in nursing animosity or registering wrong.*
>
> —Charlotte Brontë

CHAPTER SEVEN

Divorce or Death of a Spouse—Phoenix Rising

Not surprisingly, both of these events are ranked high on the stress ladder. Going through a divorce, or even worse, experiencing the death of a spouse presents any woman with a huge challenge not only to go through the process of the experience but also to start over again. Each is very tragic in its own way. Not only do you feel as if your life has been turned upside down, but you are faced with being alone. In the case of divorce, even if you look forward to it and know it is best for you, you are faced with a multitude of changes living as a single woman. When death takes a spouse you may be in despair and feel devastated at having lost your partner, whom you loved so deeply and depended on for so much; he's no longer there for you to turn to.

Although each woman's situation is individual, there are similarities when it comes to emotions and decision-making—just being becomes more unsettling. You may be thinking: "Where do I go?" "What do I do?" "What is to become of me?"

> There is an alchemy in sorrow. It can be transmuted into wisdom, which, if it does not bring joy, can yet bring happiness.
>
> —Pearl S. Buck

As we've said before—and we'll keep saying it, please be compassionate with yourself, give yourself space to feel your emotions, do your grieving, express your anger, your sadness…give freedom to all your pent-up feelings. This looks different for each woman and may be experienced like a roller coaster of emotions for some, while others might have feelings burst out and then diminish…just know that it is your experience and no one else's. It won't do you any good to compare yourself to someone else or judge yourself by how you think you "should" be handling this or how quickly you "get on with life." Getting on with life is essential yet initially it may be enough for you to simply deal with the routine activities, not taking on anything that isn't absolutely necessary, sticking to the basics and prioritizing self-care as well. There is a lot of truth in the advice to "do nothing, make no big decisions for the first six months." Or maybe even longer.

Learning to let go and cherish the special memories you had with your husband rather than clinging on is so valuable. There are some things we cannot change yet we do have a choice: We can fight it or we can learn to accept it. If you find yourself fighting it, look for a new way to view it, pulling as much positive into the situation as you can. It will serve as an opening for you to move forward and make more new choices. When you remain stuck and refuse to let go of what you want, even though you know what you want isn't possible, you will feel at your lowest. The loss becomes an even greater one.

There are a couple of women we know who lost their husbands when in their fifties. Both husbands were terminally ill with gradually degenerating conditions, so it could be argued that they had plenty of time to get used to the prospect of losing their partner. Both women were the primary caregivers for their husbands and each had a special but very different relationship with her husband.

Sarah's sister had a lovely house—all she wanted in the material sense and she was indeed the queen of her castle. When her husband died after a long illness she suffered a huge loss of self-confidence during the first year and developed a heavy reliance on her grown-up children to keep her going. She was, quite naturally, afraid of making changes in her way of life—it had, after all, been like that for a very long time. She had an unchallenged belief that older widows behaved in a certain way.

Fortunately she had the benefit of Sarah, an older sister who had also trained as a coach. At no time did Sarah tell her that she was "doing it wrong" or "being anything less than she could be." Instead she gently coached her sister to take charge of her own life, to feel she could do anything she had ever wanted to do. Little by little she has come out of it, relying less and less on her children for their support, and getting stronger and stronger. Her latest craze is something she has always wanted to do: belly dancing—and she is the one encouraging her sister to join in too!

Barbara had known her husband since they were both five years old. Theirs was a close, loving relationship founded on true spiritual understanding. She also has her ninety-plus-year-old mother living with her and lends help and support to her daughter who suffers from depression. Barbara has a very philosophical view on life and yet it is one that is constantly about putting others, and not herself, first. Over the years she had consistently declined to take any vacations with friends because her husband preferred to vacation with just the two of them. She was perfectly happy with this decision. Now she has been totally able to let go of this old choice in favor of a new one. For the first time in many years she has just enjoyed a vacation with her friends.

Both of these women cherish the memories of their departed husbands and both have learned they can also move on, designing their lives in a way that works for them.

When you have lived with a spouse, you may have depended on him when making decisions, handling financial affairs, arranging household and auto repairs, etc. Even if you have not relied on him very much, now you are completely on your own. How do you handle it? Asking family and friends for help doesn't always come easy to many of us women. Some of us believe we should be able to do it on our own, that if we ask for help we are weak. In reality, it is just the opposite. Asking for help is a sign of strength, an indication that you know when you are up against something you cannot handle on your own, or even just something that will be much, much easier with help. All successful people certainly have an entire staff of experts helping them; they do not do it alone. How about you?

- *How comfortable are you asking for help?*
- *Do you ask even if you aren't comfortable with it?*
- *What is your view of showing vulnerability? By this we mean not putting up a good front when your heart is crying out to be heard.*
- *How much more can you honor people by asking for their help? Many people want to help others and it's good to remember that they can always say no. And if they do, the key is not to be attached to their response. Do not see it as a total rejection—it is merely their choice right now.*

Because of the high level of stress you may be experiencing, and possibly depression, asking for help may need to extend beyond family and friends. It may be in your best interest to seek help from a therapist since family and friends can only help to a point. All of us look to a medical doctor when we have a physical ailment, don't we? In the same way, many times we may need to look to a good therapist when going through difficult emotional times, whether because of a divorce or death of a spouse or some other matter. We do want to emphasize that when seeking a therapist it is very wise to get a referral or make certain that the therapist has the proper qualifications and a good reputation in the field. And it is very important that she or he is someone you feel comfortable with and can trust. As with everything, you can choose what is best for you.

We encourage you to ask for help and support that keeps you in the driver's seat so you avoid going to that place of helplessness and hopelessness we talked about before. Take the support of others and use it to lift you up, not keep you down and incapable of independence.

We must not ignore that for some women who are now single, it may be necessary to rejoin the workforce, return to school, or change careers. Such a necessity may seem daunting, yet it is doable when approached with an "I can do it" attitude. Others may have a desire or an urge to try something new and/or redesign their life. If you are in this category, the direction you choose to go in will matter greatly. Ask yourself some questions, such as: "What interests me?" "What am I skilled at?" "What comes naturally to me?" For some ideas you can go back to the list of ten things you've wanted to do or try in your life. Making a move of this type may truly open the door to success and a better life, as it did for Nancy.

> Nancy was in her late forties and had two children to put through college when she and her husband divorced. She knew she wasn't going to be able to rely on him for financial support and she was not employed at the time. With the increased responsibility Nancy knew she had to take action. She thought long and hard about what she could make a living at while getting some degree of job satisfaction. She was great at organizing and planning family gatherings and social parties, so she decided to start her own event planning business from her home. She told *everyone* she knew and met, and word began to travel.

Initially clients hired her for home parties. Her reputation grew and in time, corporations and organizations started hiring her for their events.

Nancy's business blossomed, and after a few years it grew to the point that she was financially able to buy a very large home. The house has a separate wing with a separate entrance that is used for her business offices. Nancy is now one of the most sought-after event planners. Her corporate clients keep coming back because she does a great job and they especially enjoy meeting in her home office. It gets them out of the corporate environment and into a serene setting to make important decisions about their events.

Creating a new life for yourself will bring you more satisfaction and aliveness. Of course, you will always have the good memories of your previous life that you can treasure—they are crucial to who you are and nothing can take them from you. You will have new experiences that will prevent you from hanging on to the past in a way that does not serve you. It is a truism that there is no way back; you must go forward, for life is about today, not yesterday.

CHAPTER EIGHT

Over the Hill?— So...Who Says?

Who knows what is right for you to pursue at this point in your life? You do, that's for sure! You may know what it is right off the top of your head, then again maybe not. On some level you *do* know. Viewed optimistically, this stage of your life may hold something very special for you, so explore, look—it might be quite juicy!

"Over the hill" is a phrase that has negative connotations. Apparently, it first appeared in the 1950s in the U.S. and related to people who were past their prime in their professional prowess. What a huge assumption! Let's look at it from our positive perspective. What a fabulous position to be in. When you have literally walked over the hill, you often have a great view of what is going on. You've had the experience of the climb, applying yourself physically, mentally, and emotionally, and now you can see so much more. See what can happen when you change your perspective—even about a well-worn and hackneyed phrase!

The negative version of "over the hill," as in "past your prime," is a myth that definitely must go! So if you carry that belief, it's definitely time to dump it, let it go...it isn't real. If you don't believe it, it cannot have an impact on you unless you choose to let it. Neither of us is prepared to buy into that term and we certainly don't carry ourselves as if we are over the hill. We are both sixty years of age as we write this book and no way are we over the hill; in many ways, we are just getting started, each one of us designing our life the way we want it! Remember, what you think shows up in your behavior. So if you carry around the negative belief about being over the hill, then you *will* be over the hill and you will project that image for others to see. It's called self-fulfilling prophecy.

> *I'm not interested in age. People who tell me their age are silly. You're as old as you feel.*
>
> —Elizabeth Arden

Ask yourself if you are being kept back by fear of the limitations of your age. If so, what are you making up about how anything you want to do will turn out? We did a training program that involved climbing trees. Beforehand we each made up stories about how difficult it was all going to be, given our age. While it was scary, the whole requirement was about self-care, not about our fear. We could venture to say that if we had been younger, we may not have done as well; our maturity gave us the wisdom to do what we needed in the way we needed while fulfilling the program requirement and having fun at the same time.

We can't emphasize enough how strongly we believe being over the hill is a myth. We both have had experiences where women and men *much* younger than us hold us in high regard. They have repeatedly expressed how much they enjoy conversation and interaction with us since we expose them to different viewpoints and perspectives. They value our relationship, are grateful to us for all the learning and growth they experience, and certainly do not view us as over the hill.

We've heard many women say they believe the young do not respect them and think they are too old.

- *What do you believe younger people think of you?*

- *What do you think of younger people? What does this tell you about your mindset? (Remember, we are not looking at "right" or "wrong"—just your insights.)*

- *If you believe younger people think you are over the hill, how much of this is "thinking" and how much is actual experience?*

- *If you've actually had a negative experience with younger people, what stage of life were they in?*
  - *What might have been the reason for their attitude?*
  - *What signals might they have been picking up from you as a result of your own thinking?*

Chances are any criticism you may have received from a younger person was nothing about you; it was about them—a reaction based on how they see themselves and where they are in their life. One thing that maturity can give you is the ability to stand strong in who you are and not get hooked by younger people's comments that could otherwise be hurtful.

This is a good place to not only bring up our age but the shape of our bodies, condition of our faces, etc. Our physical appearance is important; it shows that we care about ourselves and care how we look—yet it does not define who we *are* as a human being. A healthy approach to your appearance is as individual as anything else about you. Some of you wear makeup, have your hair colored, and maybe have had some cosmetic surgery. All of that is fine. What we are asking you to do is to check that you are keeping a balanced perspective on your looks and who you really are. In other words, if you feel better with enhancements and in general have a fair amount of self-esteem, go for it.

However, if you rely on the enhancements too strongly and believe that you are not good enough without them or can't muster enough courage to walk out the door without them, we encourage you to stop and look at what's going on inside. What makes you feel this way? We say, you are not your wrinkles, your gray hair, or your flabby thighs; you are far more than all that. You are a woman who has already come a long way and earned the right to walk tall and proud.

Given the youth-focused marketing that surrounds us, is it any surprise that many easily develop a negative self-image? It has caused us to shun the issue of aging, and we can no longer even hope to look like the gorgeous models in the magazine and TV ads. Women of our age are faced with ads about hemorrhoids, chair lifts, and anti-wrinkle cream! We are shown that beauty looks a certain way and yet we have the inevitable telltale signs of aging. We must however bear in mind that much of what we are being shown isn't real, even with the beauty of youth on their side. It's clever makeup, cosmetic surgery, botox, enhanced photography, etc. Yet the disservice this does is a tragedy because it pushes women (and very young girls) to compare their physical attributes. A particular combination of eyes, nose, mouth, and figure does not necessarily constitute true beauty. Real beauty comes from within—that's certainly our belief.

There is a poem titled "Beauty of a Woman" apparently written by Sam Levinson although often used by Audrey Hepburn. It is easily found on the Internet and it says exactly what we mean. It isn't the clothing, the shape or figure, the hair, that make a woman, but beauty is revealed in a woman's eyes and soul where one can witness her love, her caring and passionate ways. And as we grow older, this beauty also grows. Please remember that!

Can you think of a mature woman whom you know or have seen who doesn't have the perfect body or the most beautiful face, yet when she walks into a room or when she is in conversation, everyone is uplifted and engaged? This is a woman who accepts herself as she is, recognizes her inner beauty and strengths, and stands tall.

She doesn't get caught up in the messages society sends about youth, good looks, perfect weight, etc. She may even have stopped working hard at her appearance!

Where are the ads showing *this* woman, the one who has given so much to so many *and* whose age shows through with radiance, with beauty that can only come from within? Each of you has this beauty, all in your own special way. And when you are in a place of feeling good about yourself, wow, do you radiate that beauty! Know that others can penetrate the surface and value what they see deep down in you.

We aren't saying it is wrong to want to look as good as you can. We are highlighting the freedom we can feel when we acknowledge our own unique beauty—it is life changing. Simply possessing confidence about our looks radiates beauty. The fact is, there is beauty in everyone—not just the outer covering. See the beauty shine through from within and everyone looks fabulous!

EXERCISE: Finding My Inner Beauty

Find a recent snapshot of yourself when you looked radiant (probably it's a surprising one—like when you were caught out in the rainstorm, playing a game with children, or chatting animatedly with a friend). Look carefully at it and try to see what it is that makes you radiant. We bet it's not the makeup alone! As we said earlier, this is you looking and feeling fulfilled—showing the core of who you really are. What beauty! And if you claim this beauty and embrace it, ah…the possibilities that become available to you!

We would like you to think about:

- *How much are you judging yourself by the standards society has set?*

- *How much do you appreciate about yourself that is fine, as is?*

- *How much effort do you expend when buying clothes for a special event?*

- *How much care do you take when getting ready to go out to dinner or a party? How anxious are you about whether or not you look good enough?*

- *Do you find yourself being encouraged or discouraged with your looks when you see other women, particularly younger women?*

- *How about cosmetics? How much money did you spend on them last year? What's your reason for buying the cosmetics? We certainly aren't saying not to wear cosmetics, it's about something deeper: the motivation when buying the cosmetics. Are you going from one to another because of displeasure with how you look and perhaps trying to cover signs of aging? Or are you using cosmetics to accentuate your natural beauty? There's a difference!*

When you think of how our society views aging, it's obvious just how much of a generalization it is—and an inaccurate one at that! Many women do not even hit the high point in their life until they are in their mature years—we are talking satisfaction with their lifestyle or achieving a certain level within their job or career.

Jessica Tandy is an actress who comes to mind as an example. She acted for many, many years; however, the Yahoo Movies biography indicates that her career was most active when she was in her seventies and eighties. And she won her first Oscar at the age of eighty! If she had stopped acting because she thought she was too old or because she felt she had not been as successful as she could have been, she would have missed out, and so would those of us who enjoyed her most famous roles.

Eleanor Roosevelt's greatest hour of glory, for which she is long-remembered, came in 1948 when she was sixty-four. It was at this time she was at her most active and was recognized for winning passage of the United Nations Declaration of Human Rights.

Dame Judi Dench's career has increased exponentially since 1984 when she reached fifty. Her website states that her highest acclaim and success as an actress have been achieved in her mid-sixties, proving that she and other actresses do not have to end their careers because of their advancing age!

Jennifer Murray, a fifty-seven-year-old grandmother, entered the *Guinness Book of Records* when she set a speed record for flying a helicopter around the globe, covering 35,698 miles in 97 days. She hit newspaper headlines again six years later when at sixty-three she was forced into a crash landing in Antarctica while attempting a pole-to-pole record-breaking attempt. She suffered a dislocated elbow…and is not deterred.

The point is, no matter what we would like in our lives, age is not an indicator of capability. As we move on we hope you have joined us, if you hadn't already, in dumping the idea of being over the hill—realizing what a myth it truly is! In no way could any of the women mentioned above be considered beyond their prime…it seems to us that they were or are *in* their prime.

CHAPTER NINE

If Not Now, When?

W e've talked about some of the key life situations that make this *the* time of your life and there no doubt are others we haven't covered. Regardless, a big question for you to ponder is "If not now, when?" That's it…*now* is the time; *now* is what is here, it's what we have. Life is precious and glorious and we deserve to live it fully and not keep putting "it" off. In fact, what *good* reason is there to put off a more satisfying and fulfilling life? For wherever you are on your journey, there is *more*!

Think very seriously about this following quote:

> *It's only when we truly know and understand that we have a limited time on earth—and that we have no way of knowing when our time is up—that we will begin to live each day to the fullest, as if it was the only one we had.*
>
> —Elisabeth Kübler-Ross

Do you live each day to the fullest? If not, what stops you? Look back over the years and also take a close look at the present. Do you notice if you've said or are still saying, "when…, then…"? The type of conversation you have with yourself could sound like, "When I have more time, I'll take that art

class"..."When I have more money, I'll take my dream trip to Hawaii."
Here's an opportunity to ask yourself:

- *What have I put aside?*
- *Is there something I keep promising myself I will do when...?*

So, when *will* you do it? If the "then" hasn't yet occurred, how much longer are you going to wait?

What's the negative perspective that is holding you back? Is there a critical voice inside telling you all the reasons you must wait? Many times the "when..., then..." is an avoidance. Might there be a fear that you will be disappointed, that it won't be the way you want it or you aren't capable of doing it? Do you spend time convincing yourself this "unknown experience" might not be what you want? Or are you waiting for someone to say it's OK and give you a push? Is it not OK for you to take the move on your own? Does it feel safer to stay put?

Take a close look at the reasons or "excuses" you are using. There is one thing for certain, change will occur in your life whether you choose it or not; nothing remains the same. So go for the changes you want!

Delaying and delaying a dream or desire is a sign of resistance, of denial. What are you trying to avoid? What you desire will never happen unless you take a stand and commit...commit to yourself. You need not commit to anyone else...you are the one we are talking about here.

There's a great quote attributed to Goethe that speaks to this:

At the moment of commitment,
the Universe conspires to assist you.

Yes, this is so true—we've seen it occur time and time again in the lives of our clients, friends, and in our own lives. Once you know what you want, where you are heading, and fully commit, it is surprising how the path opens up.

There's a term "life happens," which means things will get in your way, take up your time and attention, and so make it very easy to find a reason to delay putting a desire or dream into action. The only thing you can do is to allow life to happen *and* move forward through that life with what brings you fulfillment. Yes, there will be obstacles to navigate at times, and we say it is crucial to sustain that commitment, maintain an open mind, and keep on the lookout for those opportunities that let you stay or get back on track.

Alice is a colleague who has become a friend over a period of time. She has worked as an independent consultant for many years and it has only recently come to light that she has been relying heavily on third-party contracts because of her low self-esteem (albeit well hidden). She had not stepped into the powerful person she is, believing that one day it would all be possible—in her case when her husband's second career training was completed, then when he got a better position, then when he became a partner in the law firm, etc.

Recently she realized that she was doing nothing but waiting, using it as an excuse. This realization led her to take a stand for herself. With total commitment, she redesigned her own company, giving it a new name, a new purpose, a new website, and for the first time in her life as a self-employed person she said no to a third-party contract. She is going it alone, believing in herself and the beauty of what she has to offer.

The key is to dream and then commit to making your dream become real. Later on we'll touch on seeing the essence of your dream.

EXERCISE: Dreaming and Committing

- *Name one thing you want in your life. (If you have difficulty with this, imagine that you have not pursued your dream and you are at the end of your life or you have been stricken with a major illness that will prevent you from the realizing the dream. How much regret will you have?)*

- *Take a sheet of paper and start listing all of your reasons/excuses for not getting or having what you want. Let loose with this. Write down the silliest excuses you could ever imagine along with the ones that you tend to believe in. If you approach this playfully, the humorous excuses will begin to open your eyes to how invalid your other reasons actually are. Here's where you can start to dispel the fears and false ideas.*

  Once you break your way through all the excuses, then it's time to make a firm commitment. Commitment is key. If on some level you have too many doubts and are thinking that you may back out, then you are not fully committed. Remember the Goethe quote. The universe responds when we commit—but the universe gets a mixed message when we are wavering too much.

- *Start with that vision of what you want; see it, feel it, taste it…get as clear as you can on what it is. Then determine what your first steps are…do not try to figure out "how" it will all come together in the end because that's when the mind starts finding excuses again. Trust that if you put one foot in front of the other you will get there!*

  If you are feeling that this is too big a step, don't worry. As you read on it will get smaller and smaller. Or if you are thinking this all sounds hypothetical, let's share with you how our vision led us to commitment accompanied by such a large number of unknowns that it would have been very easy to walk away saying, "Nice idea, but.…"

When we came up with the idea to write a book, we had no idea at all how it would all come together…we hadn't a clue.

We started with a vision…seeing more mature women living fully in their own authenticity and power. This is something we knew we felt very strongly about and we wanted it to happen.

Once we both said a resounding *yes* to coauthoring the book, synchronicity set in:

- Someone who had just written a book showed up.
- He recommended a book coach.
- We decided to take the plunge and consult with her and before we knew it we were off on this new venture together.

And we both were firmly committed to this…there was no sitting on the fence, so to speak. We hope that as we share our passion for life and the possibilities and opportunities we believe exist for women that you, the reader, will find something of value that helps you move forward in your life too.

As we write these words for the first time, we have no idea how they will be finalized, published, etc. We certainly had no clue when we began as to how we were going to work closely together, divided by thousands of miles and a huge ocean. We are however committed to taking one step at a time. Based on what we've said earlier, we are walking our talk. And what is so important to share with you is that taking one step at a time is quite freeing. Yes, there is freedom when we stop trying to figure out how everything will be in the future. There are so many unknowns and we'd get bogged down if we allowed ourselves to spend time thinking about "how this" and "how that" in terms of this book. We'd be wasting our time and going in circles instead of writing.

This is a huge lesson for all. Stay with what is in front of you and maybe just a few steps ahead, and trust absolutely that all will be revealed when the time is right.

So, as we prepare to move on to the next section of this book, what are we saying? That regardless of where you are in your life, you always have a choice; that the time to make that vital choice for change truly is *now*.

Take one day at a time making the best choices you can. Set your goals and take action today. Yesterday is gone and you can't change it; tomorrow isn't here yet so don't try living in the future and end up forgetting today. Stay in the present knowing that what you choose today influences what tomorrow brings.

Oprah Winfrey stated it quite well:

> *My philosophy is that not only are you responsible for your life, but doing the best at this moment puts you in the best place for the next moment.*

What do *you* want to choose for today? Where are you heading for tomorrow?

Once your choice is made, the path begins. The choice is never "right" or "wrong," merely the choice you have made. Always remember that you can make another choice if you don't like the first one you've made. You will be more empowered than ever before when making conscious choices that work for you—*conscious choices that lead you to that richer, more fulfilling life we talk about!*

Tapping Into Your Energies

Take a Closer Look

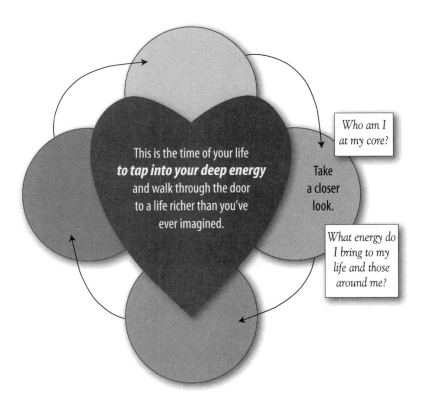

Congratulations! You are entering the second part of this book, which focuses on appreciating more and more about yourself by helping you tap into your own, personal deep energy.

There is a fountain of youth: it is your mind, your talents, the creativity you bring to your life and the lives of the people you love. When you learn to tap this source, you will truly have defeated age.

—Sophia Loren

CHAPTER TEN

What Is Deep Energy?

This section has been designed to take some different perspectives on your wisdom and energy, which *are rich gifts* to be treasured and used to advantage—both in service of yourself and those who are part of your life. We look at how to give real value to the range of energies that can be brought fully into play in your life and the best thing is, it's not about figuring it out logically.

As we take on more years, we often feel we don't have as much energy. Here we want to talk about energy in a distinctive way—energy that lives at a deep level within us. Generally the word energy brings to mind the physical energy that has us exercise, tackle a project, get through our workday, etc. And for the most part we tend to feel this "get up and go" energy is separate from our other characteristics, and at any given time we either have enough of it or we don't. However, this physical energy, along with "other" energy, is linked to every aspect that makes up who we are. And this is what we are emphasizing. It is not a myth—we are total energy!

This energy, which lives at a deep level within us, has many facets: spiritual energy, communicative or relationship energy, as well as the physical or body energy. Some people call this connected energy "wisdom," "inner knowing," "intuition," and "instinct." Although there are many different words used to identify it, we do know that it is present in everyone regardless of their age, and regrettably, most of the time it's ignored or smothered over. It is something you know with the whole of your being—not just your brain. The expression "gut feeling" didn't come from nowhere—and this is only a small part of what we are talking about.

Tapping into that energy truly becomes possible as we get more and more comfortable in our own shoes. We like to think of it as a reservoir of resourcefulness and strength that is beyond the physical and certainly beyond what you intellectually know.

So, we are going to explore some of those facets with you, to enable you to start checking in on yourself and allowing your deep energy to come through in all its different forms. As this deep energy surfaces, you will gain more self-assurance and acceptance of who you are and find greater aliveness.

Wise Through Experience

First of all, let's look at the notion of wisdom. Wisdom has long been associated with the onset of old age. People who have reached, or are approaching, retirement age have generally been regarded as older and wiser, and this tends to mean that we have gained a whole range of life experiences and supposedly learned a great deal in the process. Sometimes the mess of life seems to leave us little space to learn, and yet learning and personal growth are vital if we are to claim to have this type of wisdom. We can only claim to be wise if we have truly learned from our experiences, surroundings, and purposeful studies and we apply what we have learned wisely. It's not a rite of age.

> *Maturity isn't a product of growing older. It's a product of growing wiser.*
>
> —Ann Landers

One of the key aspects of our life experience is the learning it has given us. Some of that learning has come in a sporadic way according to what life has presented to us. Other learning may have been much more orderly and specific. We mean the classes you have attended, the qualifications you have gained, and the training you have had during your life. How much of this is genuinely of use to you? How much do you use on a day-to-day basis without even thinking about it?

By the time we get to fifty or more we have had the opportunity to become as well read as we want to be at this stage in our life. If you are saying no to yourself in your head as you are reading this, what's the no about? Is it that you haven't taken the time or that you believe you can never be as well read as you want to be? That there are loads and loads of books that you've bought but never read? What you have done though is become as well read as you *chose* to become. And you have the opportunity to turn up the volume even more on your reading, acquisition of knowledge, and powers of communication if you want to. In this phase of our life it is not uncommon for us to have the desire to know more about topics that did not appeal to us very much when we were younger. Other things were higher on our list of priorities earlier in our lives. If you so choose, the opportunity is here; it's a great time to reprioritize and catch up on the issues and subjects that attract you now.

Don't forget too that you may be judging yourself, maybe a bit harshly, when thinking of how well read you are or aren't. If so, stop to think. You may actually be more well read than you give yourself credit for. It could be that your standards are based on comparison with other people you know or on extremely high expectations of yourself that have been there for a very long time, or even a story you are making up about what well read actually means. All these perspectives are worth considering if you are to take a new look at where you stand in your own well-read stakes.

What we are increasingly realizing about this so-called knowledge-based society is that the knowledge per se is not the most important ingredient. Thanks to devices like the Internet, facts and figures can be found very quickly. It is in fact the skills that we have at our disposal that are of greatest importance. So, look at the skills you use on a daily basis that have been very valuable to you and continue to be so. Powers of analysis and synthesis, the ability to evaluate what is right for you, or not—these are skills that can definitely be learned through training and experience.

Even if you are reading this thinking you didn't finish your education and have not had very much training, you are nevertheless carrying a wide range of skills with you.

Lynn's Story:

For years as an educator in adult education, I have advised, cajoled, and persuaded women that despite their apparent lack of qualifications, they are in the perfect position to pursue the career they want. I have dealt with many women who have been caregivers and homemakers and believed that they had little to offer any employer in the job market, lacking professional qualifications or career experiences. What I was determined to have them realize was that homemaking and caring are two of the most complex jobs requiring a range of skills that would make many successful managers pale. Valuing this experience is the first step for many women toward fulfilling a dream, making a significant change in their life—even starting a new career.

Julie's Story:

I was a full-time mother and homemaker for almost twenty years before I went back out into the workforce. I was certain I didn't measure up and yet what I discovered is that my years of running a household and managing all the affairs of a family provided invaluable skills and knowledge. Actually I had acquired skills that no school or seminar could have ever taught me. My first job was as an office manager for a small business and within five years I was an account manager responsible for $60 million worth of business for a large company that supplied parts to the automobile manufacturers. Most of my friends were stunned; in their eyes I went from being a "housewife" to holding a position alongside men with many years of experience in the industry. *And* I was in my mid-to-late forties when I did this.

If on the other hand you are reading this with several degrees and a good deal of formal education under your belt, we are not discounting any of it! To be sure, everything you have attained in the form of acquired knowledge is of value—some of it in the specific field of study you chose and some of it as applied to other areas. As a simple example, if you have a degree in psychology, that knowledge is not only useful in that field but also in public relations, in personal matters, in running your own business, in developing and maintaining relationships, etc. As we've said in earlier parts of this book, all that you have learned can be utilized to benefit you—you need only keep looking!

EXERCISE: Life's Highlights

Think of different incidents in your life—some you might have classified as "good," and some you would put in the "bad" category.

- *What did you learn from these experiences?*

- *What would you say was "useful learning"?*

- *How did you incorporate that learning into your life?*

- *What learning actually does not serve you at all? (By this we mean the sort of learning that leaves you less than you want to be—perhaps it's not trusting, not risking, playing it safe, limiting yourself in what you would like to do or be.)*

Using the valuable learning allows you to draw upon the experiences of your life to feel wise.

Do a timeline of the highlights in your life—your age and what you accomplished or learned. Include marriage, birth of children, new jobs or careers, education, etc. (A timeline form is below for your use.) As you look at this timeline, what stands out about yourself? What strengths and abilities did you exhibit that allowed the highlights to occur? Be very thorough with this exercise so you will truly see as much as possible about yourself and not leave anything out.

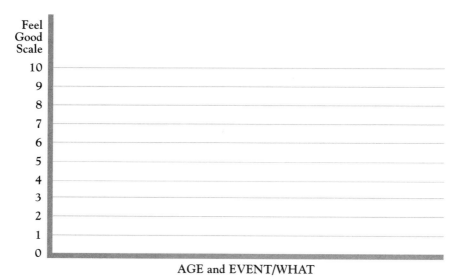

Feel Good Scale

AGE and EVENT/WHAT

We will both admit to having thought "Everybody knows what I know… everybody can do what I can." And we know that is not true. What happens is that we women don't realize how much we have accomplished. We don't recognize our wisdom because we are so accustomed to what we know and what we don't know, it seems common to us. No one has lived the same life you have, so no one knows exactly what you know. Think about it…what are you now uncovering about your wisdom?

Once you have unearthed more of your strengths and talents from this exercise, you can consciously begin to utilize them in various situations and draw upon them to increase your self-confidence. The more you are aware of, the more you have at your disposal for your benefit as well as the benefit of others. The wisdom you have acquired is priceless—do not discount anything!

Wise Through Inner Knowing

There is also another kind of wisdom that lives deep inside of you. It's that "knowing"—often called intuition or "gut" feeling—that has been there your entire life and sadly is little appreciated by our society. We are told and therefore learn to feel much more secure with analysis, information and evidence that what we are doing or going to do is "right." This results in our suppressing this inner knowing. We invite you to call this wisdom forth even more than you may have been doing. It's a great and reliable sense that we are endowed with, and one of the delightful things is that it is never too late for us to practice with it so that it becomes stronger.

If the idea of intuition or gut feeling is something you are skeptical about, perhaps this bit of information may help. It is scientifically documented that we have brain cells in our gut and those brain cells are the *first* to pick up information....Only *then* is the information received by our brain. If this boggles your mind, check it out—it is true!

Imagine what is available to us "in our wisdom" when we combine the experience of the years with our natural inner knowing. Boy! Can we be powerful in our decision-making! How wise we can be about our life when we listen to this wisdom, rather than getting hooked again by those "ought to do's" and "should do's"! Many people talk about following their path. For some it means a particular vocation—for many others it means just going with what feels right *to* them, *for* them.

What else could be available to you in your life if you ventured to use your intuition and experience more, if you truly believed in your own knowing?

Grace, one of our fifty-plus clients, used to spend a great deal of time preparing for meetings, for presentations—indeed for anything at all. She would feel bombarded by information and always be drawn to take some more files with her...just in case!

Her reaction to a challenge we put to her of not preparing at all for the meetings she had in the coming week was "No way!" Preparation was her security blanket and her fear did not allow her to recognize and own the vast experience and wisdom she already possessed. Furthermore, she had not recognized that the reason corporations were buying her services was her "knowing-ness," not the amount of preparation she was putting in.

Anyhow, she agreed—with a good degree of trepidation on her part—to not prepare at all for 50 percent of the meetings. She was amazed just how well the meetings went. She was able to access her wisdom and experience as a vital resource without her preparations getting in the way.

Grace has continued to believe that she knows what she knows…and now recognizes when preparation is necessary and when it is only a security blanket. Imagine the extra freedom she has found, the amount of clutter she has been able to throw away, and the increase in her own self-belief!

EXERCISE: Check On Inner Knowing

Here's an opportunity for you to listen for a few minutes to your inner wisdom telling you what you "know." You will need to put aside your judgments about how good or right or appropriate or big or small the messages you receive are. These are just your own self-doubting thoughts getting in the way!

Have a piece of paper and pen handy—you'll need it later. Make sure you won't be interrupted for 10–15 minutes.

Sit comfortably, play some relaxing music if you wish, and imagine going deep inside yourself…then just hang around there with the question, "What do I know?" After two or three minutes, write down anything that came to you during those few minutes. Yes, write down anything at all. This genuinely is about no judgment. There will be some pearls or insights in there for you.

If you just did the above exercise and found yourself drawn to judgment, what do you think that was about? Did you begin to wonder or worry:

- *What others might think?*

- *How your partner/son/daughter/best friend might comment if they knew you were doing this?*

- *That the answer(s) you received couldn't possibly be true or real?*

How many things are you hanging on to that you think you're no good at? This question depends on where your baseline is...and yes, it is your baseline, not someone else's!

This exercise is about following through on your inner messages and using them in your day-to-day life. Consider this: If you are finding it difficult to write down what you heard, how much more difficult is it to actually take action or fully accept who you are at your core?

There are other opportunities for you to learn to listen to your intuition, and we encourage you to practice during the course of your day and have fun with it. Pay special attention to the random thoughts, ideas, and urges that seem to pop into your head from nowhere. Do you ever experience, perhaps while driving or in the midst of another task, a totally unrelated thought entering your mind? Follow through on the thought or the urge to see if there is something there. Our analytical thinking is not always able to make sense of the thought or impulse because it is not originating in the analytical part of our brain. It is arising from another place. If you are not able to figure out what the impulse means, do not let that stop you from checking it out; there may be some value or learning for you. And if you approach it lightheartedly, you will be sure to have some fun. Your inner wisdom is always right; that is, it is always trying to tell you something. What we are sometimes not so good at is the interpretation part. And that's just fine too. Simply listen and get familiar with that inner voice all over again.

Julie:

An example is an experience my daughter Michelle had a few years ago. She was driving from one business meeting to another and was nearing a large shopping mall on the other side of town from where she lived. Suddenly for a reason unknown to her, she felt a strong urge to go into that mall and into a specific dress shop. She felt major turmoil because she did not want to risk being late for her meeting and certainly had no intention of shopping. Known to trust her instincts, Michelle just *had* to check it out so she made a quick stop and went into the shop.

As she entered the door, right there in front of her was a formal dress in the exact color, length, and size she needed. Michelle was to be the maid of honor at her friend's wedding and her friend had dreamed of Michelle wearing this precise color. However, since Michelle is *very* tall, she had not been able to find a dress long enough in that color and had purchased a different gown in a different color. What a delight for her and the bride that she followed that urge! We all smiled broadly when Michelle walked down the chapel aisle in that perfect-color gown that fit her like a glove!

Ann, another friend of ours we met in our leadership program, has a brilliant imagination. She spent many years talking endlessly with great enthusiasm about her dreams, often seeing where things could be made better. And she actually had a marvelous invention that she wanted to bring to life. But what did she do about all this? Absolutely nothing! What stopped her? On the surface, Ann's life was very successful. She was a mother and wife plus held a good job outside the home. However, Ann always placed the needs of others first and convinced herself that she had to remain at her play-it-safe job. Her salary was extremely persuasive and so was that little voice that told her she could never bring a world-changing invention to market.

When Ann started the leadership program, she described that she felt like "a racehorse stuck in the stall." She was dying to get out and run—yet didn't know how; she was afraid to face the challenge. Ironically, her desire to put others first is what enabled her to take the first step out of the stall. Her daughter's approaching wedding provided sufficient motivation for Ann to resign from the lucrative but dead-end job.

As Ann's self-esteem grew through the leadership program, she began to listen to her own inner wisdom—her intuition. She began to use positive self-talk techniques on a regular basis. Her biggest dream was the invention—a device to warm the mammogram machine surface, making the process more comfortable. Ann let nothing dissuade her; this dream became such a persistent drive that one synchronistic event after another began to occur. All that Ann needed started showing up: a patent attorney, a prototype developer, a second prototype developer, a patent process mentor, business space, marketing expertise—even funding! Every time she reached out for information, it came.

Ann became the first-place winner of the Whirlpool Brand Mother of Invention Grant and was nominated for the Innovator Award in her city.

Ann's dream has become a reality because she followed her instincts and continues to believe her invention will be of value to women around the world. No matter what obstacles arise (and they do), Ann remains focused and undeterred. Her product is now ready for marketing!

After having explored the various aspects of wisdom, we return to what we mentioned earlier—that we genuinely are unique in this world. It may sound like something of a cliché and yet it is so true.

No one else has exactly what you have to offer, and yet you may be led to believe that you should be aiming toward a standard rather than owning who you really are. You can choose to see the advancing years either as an opportunity or as a threat; you can choose to converge toward the grayness of the masses, or diverge into truly letting your own unique colors show through. As so famously stated in the poem "The Warning" by UK poet Jenny Joseph, you can give yourself permission to wear "purple with a red hat," either metaphorically or literally if you wish! You can choose to shake off the shackles of "responsible adulthood" and, if you wish, access your desire to be more outlandish, more whacky, more forgetful. In fact, more of whatever you choose! It's well worth remembering that no one else on this earth can live your life—it is totally yours—and so therefore you must make your own choices, for that is what shapes your life your way.

Let's take a look at the company you keep and how much you may or may not be paying attention to your wisdom in this area.

There is no doubt that we humans are social animals. However, we do not have the herding or flock instinct, though this is not always apparent. Old patterns and habits tend to attract or draw us to certain types of people and communities where we do not allow our uniqueness to shine through. These habits disguise the fact that we are actually "choosing"—it doesn't matter that we are unaware, we are still making a choice. Even when we avoid making a decision, we are then making the choice to not decide. Therefore what is truly important is to recognize that we are *choosing* to spend time with a given group of people, we are *choosing* our activities, our behavior, and how we spend our time. Yes, at work we don't always have that personal choice. The choice we do have however is how we choose to see the people we work with and how we choose to view our work/job/career.

Genuine choice exists in the friends you choose, the people whose company you keep, in the activities you pursue and how you choose to put these activities to use. Let your wisdom be your guide—trust it!

We so often hear women saying, "Oh, I've got to look after the grandchildren this week so I won't be able to make it." What mysteries are contained in the phrase "got to"? It's an interesting one, isn't it, because it's very much a part of the language. "Got to"—does that mean there's a rule? An expectation on the part of your son or daughter or your own expectation from what you were taught? A rut you've fallen into? Or is it simply a habit of words? Perhaps you are consciously choosing to look after the grandchildren this week. If so, why not practice saying it? See how different you feel when you express it as a choice, rather than a "got to."

During the course of the next few days notice how often you say—either out loud or to yourself (and there are great "got to" conversations that go on with ourselves!)—"I've got to…go to a meeting/do the grocery shopping/make the dinner/see a client/have drinks/look after the dog, etc." Then practice shifting to words of choice and see how different it feels.

There may be occasions when "got to" does feel like there's no choice. Notice what is going on in your body when you say yes and you actually want to say no. The no is coming from your deep wisdom, of knowing that there is something else for you, some other choice to be made. Test it out—do not deny that voice of knowing; pluck up the courage and actually say no. We can assure you that the world won't fall apart! Yes, it may be messy insofar as the other party might be thrown, angry, hurt, but then again let's not make assumptions. The other party may be quite OK with your choice. You won't know until you do it. Fulfilling your own life is not always easy; nevertheless, you thoroughly deserve it.

If we do not allow ourselves to say no, to do what is best for us, to choose for ourselves, to honor our individuality, we denounce the essence of who we are. How often do we take up a line of study or an activity because it's what a friend has done or is doing? That's not to deny it can be interesting or right for us. What we often do is fail to put our wisdom and learning into practice in a way that is best for us. We tend to get swayed by following the well-trodden path, no matter how uncomfortable it may feel. Whether it's learning how to embroider or do physics, speak another language or scuba-dive, when we listen to our wisdom, we can sense what we want to do with our new learning, rather than what is expected of us. We can follow our own specific path.

Lynn:

Over the past few years as I've gone through a number of changes I've noticed myself being drawn at one level to "doing it right" according to textbooks, or as other people see it. At another level I've always known that if I listen to myself I'll find the way that works for me.

So, here are the kinds of tension between "should do" and "know what works" I've been working with:

- As a person who runs her own business, I have always found myself resisting doing a business plan of how I am going to develop a particular aspect of my company even though all the advice you get is to "start with a business plan."

- I believed that as I entered coaching I had to leave my world of education behind—and yet I knew the pull was still there. When I detached myself from this belief, my clients appeared—from the world of education.

- When I did my MBA I had no idea how I was going to use it; when I started coaching training I had no idea how I was going to use it, what my niche was going to be…and I still don't!

What I have realized is that I can design my knowing in any way that works for me and honors the values I have of variety, serendipity, connectedness, and spontaneity. People may see me as something of a maverick—so what!

CHAPTER ELEVEN

Physical Energy—
Deserving and Serving

W e've taken a look at what we mean by the form of deep energy we know as wisdom that is constantly available to us. We are now going to turn our attention to the form of energy that we referred to earlier as the one that springs to mind first of all—physical energy. The stuff that has us bounce out of bed in the morning, or crawl out of bed; the stuff people sometimes are out to convince us that as we get older we have less of it. We know this not to be true—it just starts to look a different way and needs nurturing in a different way.

In Section One we pointed to the fact that as women we spend a lot of our lives putting ourselves at the bottom of the list as far as self-care is concerned: when there's an epidemic of flu in the family and the kids get the attention; the need to go and check on Mom and Dad after a hard day's work; the need to catch up with the housework on the weekend after working all week. As we progress through life, our needs change. Perhaps in our twenties or thirties we were fine with burning the candle at both ends, even prided ourselves at being capable of it. Although it may have seemed fine, it wasn't—it never is in our best interest at any stage of life. So if you haven't already, it is crucial to reassess what your real needs are and to be aware that they may vary as the conditions in your life change. With that said, how often do you put *your* needs, *your* health, and *your* well-being as far up on the list as you place everyone else's? Is there a belief about deserving or earning that gets in your way? For most of us there is—or at least there has been in the past.

So here's a lesson on deserving. We're going to abandon an old lesson you may be carrying with you that you need to "earn" in order to "deserve" a treat like a long soak in the tub accompanied by relaxing music and a glass of wine. Instead we're going to see ourselves as already deserving so that we can remain in service to humanity. Now it's time to walk the talk. The one thing we are very good at is giving advice to our friends, to our daughters, sisters, nieces about what they need to do to sustain their physical energy. The truth is, we are *all* deserving, regardless of who we are or what we do. How about self-care? What do *you* need to rejuvenate and sustain your energy?

The word self-care is translated by some to mean "selfish." Yet self-care is *not* selfish. As we have said before, it must come first. We cannot fill another's cup if our own is empty. We may fool ourselves into thinking we can. However it is not possible to give to others what we do not have ourselves. First off, we need to know just what will fill our cup of physical energy by listening carefully to our body and the wisdom that it holds. Don't you just know when it is more appropriate for you to stay in bed an extra hour or so or when it is better to get up and go for a brisk walk; when a bike ride is just the ticket or when it's a good idea to put your feet up and listen to music? How often do you discount these internal messages because guilt creeps in and you believe there is so much you must do that you cannot give yourself the much-needed break? Ignoring these messages works against us by depleting our energy and/or negatively affecting our health.

Listening carefully and responding to what our body is telling us is exactly what allows us to maintain and increase our own physical health and capacity. How much self-care do you practice? When was the last time you had a massage or a pamper session? Perhaps you have always wanted to have a Reiki session, try yoga or Pilates. Listen to your body! Is it calling you to try something new? Remember, you are already deserving. You've waited long enough; go ahead, give it a go—it could make all the difference! Chances are you will feel refreshed and just maybe you will begin to realize that self-care is *not* selfish! And, by the way, what have you got to lose anyway? In the grand scheme of things, an hour or two is nothing!

EXERCISE: Caring About Me!

Here is a short exercise that will help you commit to action around your own self-care.

Fill in the blanks in the statements given below:

- *Here are five things for my greater self-care I am committing to over the next month:*

    1. _____
    2. _____
    3. _____
    4. _____
    5. _____

- *In terms of self-care, I've always wanted to _____.*
    (Do any of your dreams from your list of ten apply here?)

- *I shall fulfill this dream by [insert a date that works for you].*

- *To fulfill this dream, these are the steps I need to take (list as many steps as you need):*

    1. _____
    2. _____
    3. _____
    4. _____
    5. _____

Transfer these commitments to your journal and put them on your calendar…now!

It is important to get very clear on another aspect that is tied in to self-care: when we are pacing ourselves and when we are stretching ourselves. The truth is that we need a balance of both and what is pacing for one person will be a stretch for another. We women tend to be very practiced in moving swiftly from one job to the next, from one chore to the next. Pacing ourselves to take time out— maybe just to smell the roses in the garden, listen to the sounds of nature, whatever turns you on—is essential. Being conscious of what is going on for us in any given moment is crucially important. You may miss something that will make your day. It also means that you will probably get those jobs done faster anyway because you'll be revitalized instead of worn out

Lynn:

At the age of fifty-eight I decided to walk my first marathon to raise funds for charity. Walking—yes—the full 26.2 miles—yes. This was a mega challenge I felt called to do, and so I had to start understanding the difference between pace and stretch and also what sustaining physical energy really meant to me. First, I enlisted two very willing helpers—my two dogs; then I set up a regimen that worked for me. Knowing how many miles beforehand just did not do the job. What did work was gradually extending the time spent walking and then calculating how far I had walked afterward. Nor did I cope particularly well with a walk that went just there and back—it had to be either circular or one-way, in which case I needed to be picked up. This meant enlisting the help of my husband, who was a willing chauffeur.

I decided I would walk to my masseuse—or at least as far as I could get in the time I allocated myself—once a week.

The whole thing worked beautifully. I fulfilled a challenge and completed the course faster than I could ever have dreamt of in a thousand years.

So here we are back again to listening carefully to the physical wisdom that our body holds. How much notice do you take of the messages your body is sending you? Thirsty? Do you have a habit of preparing coffee or do you listen to your body? Maybe it's asking for plain old water. Or a cool glass of wine! Honor your body as if it were a friend—for that's exactly what it is, and as we grow older it becomes a much more special friend that needs to be truly looked after. There is an intelligence in the body; it knows what to do *and* it needs you to work with it, not against it. Be flexible and open-minded as your body's needs change through the years.

If you have spent your life being very active, even athletic, it can be frustrating when you know that you are past your peak and there is no way you can recapture those moments of youthful vitality. None of us can, not if we expect they are going to look just as they did in the past. So, yes, do grieve your loss but do not hold on to the past, because if you do, you won't allow the new to come in. Bottom line: When we cling to the past we suffer. Conversely, if we shift gears and start looking at different peaks—those that are within our pace and stretch range right now, we can enjoy a huge sense of achievement and well-being. Here is where a new perspective can help you make a huge shift. There very well may be some activities or hobbies you've never tried because you were so active or busy engaging in sports. You may not even be aware of what else is available to you. Now is the perfect time to explore a bit and try out some new activities or interests—you may find one or more that are very satisfying.

Either way, the status quo is not the way to go. The one thing about life is that it is never static, and so change is the only constant thing we know.

Is there anything you've been dying to do and never thought you'd get there? Why not give it a try! Whatever it is, go savor and enjoy it. If we spend time beating ourselves up about how much faster younger people go, how much more flexible they are, etc., our mindset won't allow enjoyment and sense of achievement to creep in…and what energy we feel when we have achieved something we set out to do!

Truth be told, younger people do not all go faster—yes, some do but some don't. You must focus on your *own* energy, not compare yourself to others. You need to take responsibility for doing the best you can to affect your energy in a positive way. That means developing the good habits of deserving and self-care, listening to your body and partnering with it, giving to yourself, exploring new interests and activities—all this will spark the life in you. Energy comes when there is excitement and full engagement in life.

CHAPTER TWELVE

Spiritual Energy—In Us and Around Us

*L*et us move from a more tangible form of energy—the physical—to one that is amorphous and therefore sometimes unnamed: spiritual energy. We have already spoken a lot about our innate inner wisdom: the inner knower that lives outside of our intellect, which, if we care to listen, can show us what is necessary for us to do for ourselves.

Looking externally at spiritual energy, the Native Americans have a phrase, "Matykea oyasin," which means "we are all related." They have clearly known something for centuries that we are only just cottoning on to. Over recent decades scientists from a range of disciplines in different parts of the world have, through their experiments, identified that fundamentally we are all made up of charged-up energy. There is a connecting energy to and between everything around us as well as within us. This is an energy over which we have no control—rather like gravity, it just is.

This energy around us is sometimes referred to as the universal mind or universal consciousness. It helps to explain how people in different parts of the world can be making the same scientific discovery at about the same time: There is a link between all of us—we are all connected by this energy. We so often hear that we are all like the waves of the ocean. Like the waves we are individuals and just like the waves that cannot be separated from the ocean, we are not separate from each other, we are one.

Taking this discussion further, we as humans are composed of energy and this energy extends out from our body. Our body is vibrating at one frequency that enables it to be seen and touched. The energy that extends beyond our body is vibrating at another frequency and usually cannot be seen, although there are people who can see this energy, which is referred to as our "aura." Our energy is interconnected with the energy of others.

It is said that newborn babies are most in tune with that energy—when there is nothing else to get in the way, we suppose. The world of a baby is very simple—the baby feels, hears, sees, smells, senses yet hasn't developed the intellect to analyze all the stimuli. Therefore the baby relies entirely on instinct and feelings. Psychologists report that a baby can sense if her mother is sad or angry even if the mother is smiling and talking gently to the baby. The baby's innate instincts are still finely tuned and therefore she picks up the unseen energy from her mother. You can't fool a baby!

As we grow we tend to lose touch with this universal energy. We are exposed to so many stimuli in the world, it is only natural that we become alienated to some things, allied to others; part of one religious group, or another, or none; affiliated to one particular political way of thinking, or another; following rules and protocols about how to behave. Is it any wonder with so many sources and so much input coming at us that we lose touch? And yet by so doing we miss out on so much energy.

What would it be like for us to get in touch again and resonate with the energy that surrounds us? In other words, let the innate wisdom inside of us be aligned with the natural energy that exists outside so that our path can become even clearer.

One of the ways of looking at this is in the terms of the physicist's "particles" and "space." Here we use it as a metaphor for what goes on in our lives. Particles are the numerous, unknowable, or unexpected events that show up in our daily life that we tend to take too seriously and give a great deal of attention to—what we might refer to as our "brain clutter." Because we focus on these particles so much, we do not see there is space for us to continue to move forward. It's quite normal for us to get enmeshed by these particles. If life is a journey, then the particles—rather like the crowds of people we may meet in the street—get in our way, make it more like walking through molasses—it's very hard work.

The next time you are at the mall, on Main Street, or anywhere it's very busy, just try walking forward intentionally knowing that space is going to open up in front of you. There is no need to be aggressive or even assertive. Just hold the intention that there will be space, and spend time looking for it. Do not get caught up thinking about the difficulty of making it through the crowd—keep your eye on where the space is. Notice how much easier it is to walk through the crowd in this manner.

What we all crave is finding that kind of space in our lives, allowing the journey to be particle-free. Yet life is messy—we can't get rid of the particles. The only thing we can do is choose how we see them.

There is no reality in the absence of observation.
—according to "The Copenhagen Interpretation
of Quantum Mechanics"

Another way of saying this is that each one of us lives in our own separate reality—we create our own reality by what we see and what we think about it.

Do you see everything as a major hitch or catastrophe? Or are you able to glide over these perceived hitches, knowing full well where you are heading, fully intentional of getting there? If you do, you will know that particles can just disappear—some you will not even notice because they are not that important. If your neighbor has bought or leased a new car and you'd like a new one too but haven't done so in years, a whole host of particles can be created: "What's she going to think about my old car?" "How can I be seen driving around in that thing when my neighbor has a new one?" "How am I going to be able to afford a new car?" And so the mental debate goes on. The simple fact is that your neighbor has a new car. After that you create your own reality—particle-full or particle-free. Again, it is your choice.

So the next time you find something getting in your way—could be some plans that are important to you and they are not falling into place as you expected (for instance, in your commitment on self-care in Chapter Eleven, have you encountered obstacles?)—look to the space. Open your mind to how you are choosing to see your issue and then see what other ways there are of looking at it. Notice what transpires when you take this position. You may not see any options at all if your attention is stuck completely on the particle that you believe is a showstopper. We can't say it enough, look to the space …it's there!

From what we've said so far, we see spiritual energy as a kind of all-embracing, quiet, and compassionate energy that at the same time brings us alive. When you can start looking for the space in your life—and you may prefer to get to this through meditation, deep reflection, or praying—you will be able to find the path that is right for you much more easily. As we've suggested several times, "going inside" is a way of quieting the mind and helps you get in touch with the space, the spiritual energy that brings you greater consciousness and clarity.

One place where women are in tune with this type of energy is in the home. We can immediately gauge the emotional climate—is it comfortable, warm, spooky, unwelcoming, etc.? The only thing we are doing is reading the energy that is around us.

The same is true when we enter a room—we can pick up the energy of what is going on in the room. Sadly, when we are younger we notice it and then forget or ignore it, especially when we are reading that something is not going too well. As we say, it is difficult to "name the elephant in the room." Our ability to sense that energy increases rather than decreases with age. Our skill at avoiding it can also increase, even though we are serving no one by doing so.

Learning to state in an effective manner what appears to be occurring will be dealt with in the next chapter on communicative energy.

What is important to keep in mind is that this all-embracing deep spiritual energy is about being aware and sensing it to the fullest. Once you've done that, you can then bring your deep wisdom into play to discover the best way to move whatever is going on forward without further conflict and with total compassion. As you get older, creating more space in your life allows plenty of room for unconditional love and compassion—even when it is combined with a passionate, principled belief.

EXERCISE: The Elephant in the Room

- *Think of a time when you entered a room of people and just "knew" that something was going on.*

- *Now think of a time when there was a strong argument or discussion going on and you knew that no one was naming the issue.*

- *Spend a few minutes considering first the actual and then possible alternative outcomes. In other words, how could these situations have come out differently?*

- *Now what about a time when you did "name the elephant in the room" when everyone else was skirting around it, pretending it wasn't there?*

- *How did it feel to name it? And what happened?*

- *If you can't think of such a time, what stopped you?*

It's a good idea to journal your thoughts for this exercise. As you read through what you have written, ask yourself: How could my part in all of this have been better?

There is so much that can be said about spiritual energy since it is such an intricate part of our lives, the world, the universe. Here we want to talk about "flow." We often hear about people being "in flow" with their life. We sense this is often interpreted as everything being hunky-dory—and in our experience this is not necessarily the case. For us it is more about being OK with whatever is going on, whatever mess is being created, and being at ease with it. The spiritual energy creates the flow as long as we do not fight it. This makes life so much easier to handle than when you feel like you are pushing water uphill. Life does start to feel effortless when our internal and external spiritual energies are aligned. How do we get to that state? By accepting that life will go on regardless of what we do? Yes, in part, and more. Accepting that the only life we can influence is our own, and the way we decide to perceive it will either move us into the state of flow or not. Determining how we are going to choose to perceive what is going on for us is key. The only thing that makes us feel stuck is our own thought process. Change those thoughts and we can change our life. This may sound too easy. Let's look at an example that is personal to us.

When we set out working together we were determined we were going to run workshops for women who were approaching or past the age of fifty. Then we started meeting hurdles at every turn—not the least of which was a severe illness. We could have stayed out of alignment with what was going on and got either frustrated or angry that nothing seemed to be working for us; or we could have abandoned the idea and forgotten about it altogether. What we found ourselves doing was simply sitting with the "not knowing" for several months. The energy of the work and our inner wisdom were not in alignment and nothing was happening. So we did nothing. We didn't push each other or try to make things happen.

> As energies aligned we saw the possibility of shifting our ideas from just running workshops to writing a coaching book. It was in line with how our world was at that time…and so we went ahead.
>
> You are reading the result.

The key message of this section is for you to learn to be in the flow of your life, keeping yourself at the helm even when the seas get rough. Shifting blame on to others means only one thing: You are giving up the control of your life—you are choosing stuckness rather than flow.

Learn what your spiritual energy feels like; look for the space and feel the flow. It can be that easy.

CHAPTER THIRTEEN

Communicative Energy— What Did You Say?

One of the greatest gifts we have is the ability to communicate, the power of speech, intonation, vocabulary, not to mention a whole range of gestures and facial expressions, which, in combination, make up an infinite number of ways of transferring thought to another person. Is it any wonder that communication can also be our downfall?

EXERCISE: Habitual Sayings

Words are slippery—and we can make assumptions that what they mean to us will carry the same meaning for someone else. Family experiences and experience of the world mold our vocabulary and phraseology.

- *What are some of the phrases you have been saying for years?*
- *What do you truly mean by them?*
- *Where do you find you have difficulty being understood?*
- *What assumptions are you making?*

Let's look at "communicating with purpose." We have deep resources of communicative energy at our disposal available to us through life's experiences; observation of life; listening, thinking, and speaking. We need to make it count because where we are now in our lives gives us huge credibility and power to be heard and, more importantly, to influence our family, friends, and community— in other words our particular world, as well as the world at large. Throughout the years we have been able to get clarity about what matters most to us and sometimes we have to stand alone on that. We will not always have everyone in full agreement with us.

So, how far are you prepared to stand up and be counted? How influential are you in your world? What would you like more of? You may want your world to be bigger or to have a greater sphere of influence; or you may want greater clarity about what impact you can make in your world. Spend a few moments thinking about the impact you want to make. Remember, this isn't about comparing or imitating someone else. It's about being who you are and creating the impact you want. We'll develop this further in this chapter.

We usually do not have any idea of how other people see us and can be hugely surprised when we ask them. Even with the passing of years we still carry stories with us about what people think; how good we are or aren't; how well we engage people, or don't—all of which can be based on something that happened or was said years ago. If you don't believe us, put your hand up if you think you can't sing or aren't artistic or creative or sporty because someone told you so when you were young—just a child.

Lynn:

When I started being coached in my early fifties one of my homework assignments was to ask thirty people I knew what they found engaging about me and what they would like to see more of. I was astounded to learn what they valued in me as a friend, colleague, or just someone they knew. I had no idea I was making that kind of impression and how very clearly they were able to see my values and what makes me tick. I was amazed how many of them genuinely appreciated being asked—even though they found the question, shall we say, unusual at first.

I was so happy to have been given this opportunity to ask because I would never have thought of doing it on my own. It helped me learn what to value in myself, and what to ditch merely as stories about myself that I had been carrying with me for a very long time.

Another aspect of communicative energy is the ability to keep or create harmony. In general, we women have a tendency to be the peacemakers in our families, with our friends, and with co-workers. How many times have you noticed a chill in the air at a family gathering and found yourself initiating a pleasant conversation? What about the times members of your family (your son, daughter, husband/partner, or child) are in the midst of a hot argument and you step in to be the mediator? Then there are meetings and disagreements on the job…how often are you smoothing things out in those arenas? We are not referring to the unfortunate habit many of us have of being "people pleasers." No that is not in anyone's best interest.

Cultivating harmony and joy through compassion for ourselves and others is the natural human state and it remains strong in women. We therefore have a collective responsibility. What else can we do to further cultivate harmony—harmony that extends out beyond our personal world? If we women take a stand and model acceptance, tolerance, and peace, imagine what a snowball effect we could start. As with any transformation, it must begin with each individual; only then can it spread outward. And we can best do this by constantly accessing our inner reservoir of strength.

When an idea reaches critical mass there is no stopping the shift its presence will induce.

—Marianne Williamson

Are you willing to help create such a shift? It starts with each one of us taking one step at a time.

To what extent are you able to live side by side with your fellow humans, welcoming and accepting their unique-ness—just as you would like them to welcome and accept yours? How far does your choice of words reflect this?

• *How does your communicative energy convey the importance of acceptance in your everyday life?*

In the same way that you can choose to design your life, you can choose how you see your own reality and how you want to describe it through your choice of words and your mode of expression.

OK, how do we do this? Start with what we know to be true: The greater our sense of self, the greater our ability to be generous and compassionate with other people's views; the greater our ability to meet them where they are and so avoid unnecessary conflict. "Meet them where they are" is a phrase used to describe how we can, to some degree, look at an issue or situation through the eyes of the other person. Placing ourselves in *their* shoes, not our own, and un-derstanding what *their reality might be*.

It is true we can never know *exactly* what it is like to be in some-one else's shoes; however, we can strive to understand what the other's opinion is and *why*. Their life experiences have influenced their think-ing just like your experiences have influenced yours. Looking at a situation from someone else's frame of reference opens the way for both sides to communicate more effectively. When a person feels heard and understood, she/he is far more willing to listen and understand another person. It is only when we do this that we can start to move forward in harmony, standing shoulder to shoulder with the other person and finding the way of compromise (even if it is agreeing to disagree)—the win-win, not the lose-lose that can so often be the result.

Spend a few minutes watching the TV news or a talk show and notice how confrontation is the norm. Aggression in words and communicative actions are generally thought of as being acceptable and a part of today's world.

Still, we are the first generation where the softer, feminine expressions have been brought into general usage, even within the language of business. For example, it is quite usual to say something like "Let me share a story with you," giving you, the listener, an active part as well in the process. The whole world of customer service has been built on the need for openness and approachability. Organizations have accepted seeing themselves as having values and ethics and being caring; even the term "human resources" has a richness not contained in its predecessor, "personnel." There is a great deal more emphasis in the business world on collaboration and teamworking in order to achieve targets and less on individual heroes and conflict. We believe this is the result of more and more women taking a leading role in the shaping of their world rather than an intention to shift entrenched vocabularies.

Elaine Chao, Secretary for Labor, speaking at the Conference on Women Entrepreneurship in 2002 had the following to say in this regard:

Scientific research has shown us that women do in fact have a higher ability to collaborate with others and nurture those around them. In the workplace that translates to more teamwork and better benefits for employees.

The era of the command-and-control management model is being eclipsed by the new collaborative-management and customer-focused model. This model is proving to be more flexible, allowing American businesses to be more competitive—and therefore more successful—in the global marketplace.

The business writers are calling it the "feminization of management thinking." I like to call it being a savvy business manager and leader.

Sometimes it is difficult for us women to own this communicative energy—especially when in an environment where competition and winning is paramount. We believe that women learn to compromise very early on in life—well at the start of puberty. Compromise is not weakness. It is actually another way of being—being true to yourself and your beliefs while remaining open and willing to cooperate and collaborate with others. Nor is this a weak way of working—it is being assertive rather than aggressive. Women of our age can be particularly adept and elegant at doing this. There is a certain grace that comes from selflessness—that state of being OK with who we really are—and when this is combined with true listening it leads to conflict-free deep discourse and decisions.

> *You can stand tall without standing on someone.*
> *You can be a victor without having victims.*
>
> —Harriet Woods

How do we listen? People often describe themselves as good listeners when what they actually mean is they are good advice givers. It's worth taking time to take another look at listening. Here are a few tips.

First, there's not just one level of listening available to us. Most of the time we *listen to* other people.

Most conversations are simply monologues delivered in the presence of a witness.

—Margaret Miller

We listen to them telling their story and we are up in our heads with our own thoughts about how we feel regarding what they are saying; linking it with similar relevant experiences we've had so that we can share them as soon as the person stops talking; thinking about how to divert this boring conversation into something else. The list is endless but we think you get the drift. We are listening, yet not with full attention.

Next comes *listening for*. This time your listening is much more centered on what the other person is saying and you are not a part of it. It doesn't matter so much what you think, what similar experiences you have had. You are not caught up with your own thoughts; instead you are focused on what the speaker is saying and nothing else. This is what matters. Of course, minds wander, so a great trick when you find yourself drifting off into "me land" is to silently repeat everything the person is saying word for word. You can't think about "me" then and you'll soon be focused on the other person again. When listening in this way, you will pick up so much more of the meaning and intent of the speaker since you have eliminated the distractions of your own thoughts.

Finally, there is *listening from*. This is a combination of listening to, listening for, and something else. That something else lies in your intuition, your inner wisdom, which we have already mentioned. It's in the "what is not being said" or the "what is actually being said," when you notice that the words do not seem to match either the energy or the meaning of what is being said. Here you are listening from your own wisdom, from a place that is not judgmental. Listening in this manner will open up an entire new awareness and understanding on your part when others are talking. And when it is your turn to speak you can speak to what your intuition, as well as your ears and eyes, were telling you.

Make no judgments where you have no compassion.

—Anne McCaffrey

When you are listening *for* and *from*, you can get curious about what is being said. You can ask innocent, non-loaded questions because the answer does not matter to you. We do not mean you do not care, but that you do not have a vested interest in whatever the answer might be. The power of listening for and from can provide you with a brand new outlook and viewpoint of other people since you will begin to more accurately understand what they are actually saying.

EXERCISE: Deeper and Different Listening

Try noticing your levels of listening next time you are out with friends, or having a deep discussion or argument with your partner. You may find yourself having to let go of old ways of doing things, shifting to a place of listening without any need to have the answer or the right piece of advice. And we are pretty certain what needs to be said will come to you because you will be hearing what is being told to you. Notice how the conversation can take a different turn when listening in this way.

Here are some sample questions to ask the person you are listening to. They are open and curious—not intended to lead the person talking anywhere other than where they want to go.

- *What would you gain by choosing that solution?*
- *What other way can you look at this issue?*
- *What are you not saying?*
- *Where's the biggest struggle for you?*
- *What would give you the greatest joy in this situation?*

The list of possible questions is endless, so do try playing with some of your own.

Now, let's consider your speaking skills. How well honed are they right now?

One of the things we know is the more comfortable you are about yourself, the more impact you will have in saying what you truly have to say. To do this you need to quiet any negative thoughts, such as: "What will others think?" "What if someone gets angry?" "I don't have the right words," "It's not my place to speak," "I don't have sufficient credentials"—indeed any thought that has you think you shouldn't be speaking. These insecurities are normal *and* you don't have to live by them. Whatever you are thinking will be manifested in your behavior. Shift to a new perspective and accept that there will always be people who do not understand or will not agree with you. This does not reduce your right to speak.

We are not necessarily referring to speaking in public on a topic you're passionate about—just sitting around the family table, with your friends, or other social settings will do just fine. You need to have the energy of your communicative skills so that what you want to say matters, lands, and has the impact you intend. Your energy comes out not only in your words but also in your voice and is anchored in the whole of your body.

The moment we begin to fear the opinions of others and hesitate to tell the truth that is in us, and from motives of policy are silent when we should speak, the divine floods of light and life no longer flow into our souls.

— Elizabeth Cady Stanton

The manner in which you speak is crucial. Your life experiences have shown you that what you say and how you say it make a huge difference in the response you receive and how you may feel as a result of the response. It is one thing to be demanding and/or aggressive, and it is another to be honest and authentic. Here we are urging you to practice being straightforward and give yourself permission to do what comes naturally to you.

How direct are you in your communication when you are sharing something that is important to you or when you are asking for what you need? Do you "beat around the bush" or get specific? For instance, if you express a belief, do you preface it with disclaimers or do you end the sentence with a questioning tone in your voice as if you were seeking approval from the listener? Or, do you stand firm, clearly making your statement with intention and passion, yet in an unemotional tone of voice? That's the most effective.

One piece of advice is that you need to say exactly what you mean without going into a convincing or defensive stance. The best tone of voice to use, especially when bringing up hot topics, is the same tone you would use if you were saying, "pass the butter please" in a totally noncommittal way. Try it on with small issues—see how it feels and what response you receive. The truth is, the more you load what you have to say with emotion and judgment, the more you will get back.

The big thing is not to be attached to the outcome—let go of any expectations you might have about how people might react (positively or otherwise). The truth is their reaction is their reality—not yours. You are still responsible for your impact…you can stay around and be prepared to help clear things up if there are disagreements or hurt feelings. It's certainly not the time to withdraw or run away.

Consider this tagline to what we are talking about: full self-expression with responsibility for impact. We encourage you to be authentic and straightforward, strong and passionate in your views, but not emotive. To have the impact you intend, you must also be sensitive and respectful of the other person(s)—your listener(s). It is important to remember that speaking to someone is not a "monologue with a witness"—there is another person to consider.

Intended impact is about finding the path that allows you to say what you want and impacts the listener in such a way that the conversation can move forward in a positive manner. However, because we cannot be in another person's reality, we sometimes create an unintended impact. Sometimes what you say and mean is not what is heard and understood.

Responsibility for impact sits with both parties—the speaker and the listener(s). Communication is a two-way street. Each person needs to hold a constant awareness of the impact of their spoken word and behavior on themselves and the other party. Remaining clueless about what the response might be is a good way because it is easier to remain unattached to how someone "should" respond, and avoids the feeling of disappointment (and other negative emotions) when they don't respond the way we want. The more you incorporate judgment in what you have to say, especially judgment of those who are listening to you, the stronger the reaction is likely to be. Those listening to you will be able to pick up on your judgments whether you speak them directly or not—they will sense them through your choice of words, facial expressions, tone of voice, etc.

EXERCISE: Rewriting History

This is a good place to stop and reflect on conversations you have had over the past week or month.

- *How much permission did you give to fully express yourself, while at the same time taking responsibility for your impact?*

  For instance, if you were involved in a heated discussion or argument, did you find yourself like two people: one person with the angry, explosive words (not taking responsibility for impact); the other like an alter ego watching what was going on and noting how silly the whole thing was, how easily the whole thing could be solved?

- *What action did you take when you made this realization? What else might you have done?*

- *On a scale of 1–10, how effective overall have you been at full self-expression with responsibility for your impact in creating good win-win situations?*

Take time to journal your thoughts. You could even rewrite history and revisit a particular conversation, making it work out better through your new approach.

When you take responsibility, you stay fully aware of what is going on, not just for yourself but also for the people you are addressing. If you practice this way of communicating, in time it can become natural and comfortable to you.

Genevieve, a friend of ours, was at a large banquet and was talking with the person sitting next to her at the dinner table on a subject she is passionate about—the inner wisdom of children and the three principles of Mind, Consciousness, and Thought. Now, you need to understand that you cannot fail to notice passion in Genevieve. It exudes from every pore in her body! She suddenly became aware that there was silence all around her—her passion had become tangible in the room and others had ceased their conversations to listen to what she had to say.

She was not putting on a performance, nor intending to be overheard—she was merely giving herself full permission for self-expression of what she believes in, spoken from the heart, and she was totally responsible for her impact. She just kept going and allowed others to listen, ask questions, and join in the conversation. Her impact was probably even greater than if she had stood up and addressed the whole room.

The next story happened when we were meeting over a cup of coffee. Elaine has a great sense of humor and when approached by a zealous waiter to take her cup away she feigned offense with twinkling eyes, indicating that she'd not finished yet. We know her and sensed what she was doing. However, it was obvious from the waiter's demeanor that her intended impact had landed badly—a mess had been created and needed cleaning up. So, as soon as she finished her cup of coffee, she got up and returned the cup to the waiter so she could communicate with him and get to a win-win situation. The end result was a smiling waiter and a smiling friend. Without Elaine's taking responsibility for her impact, the story could have been very different.

It is important to note that she did not approach her "mess clearance" with groveling apologies but a lighthearted approach that transferred to the waiter. She trusted her intuition that this was what was needed in this circumstance. While it is true that the waiter's reaction was his problem (he may have been having a bad day; not feeling well—a myriad of possibilities) Elaine's willingness to clear up the mess helped the waiter learn and made it good for all concerned.

This chapter has given you a sense of how much richer and fulfilling relationships can be when we are able to create a positive communication spiral while still saying what we want, listening fully to what others have to say, and being willing to own our impact. As you learn to create positive communication in this way, other people will learn much from you.

CHAPTER FOURTEEN

Values—Your Energy Trigger

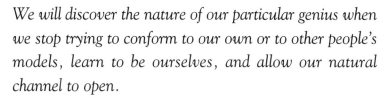

We will discover the nature of our particular genius when we stop trying to conform to our own or to other people's models, learn to be ourselves, and allow our natural channel to open.

—Shakti Gawain

Think of the times when you felt really, really alive. It does not have to be a hugely happy occasion. Indeed, some of our peak moments are when they are full of ordeal or stress—such as competing for an important job, winning a cake-baking competition, or running a race. When we are in such moments, all that we hold dear to us in our very core is being honored or aligned. These are the values that have us get out of bed in the morning and feel good about our journey on the river of life, regardless of whether we are in the rapids, in a quiet eddy, or just cruising along.

We are fortunate to have reached half a century or more in our lives and can enjoy a huge array of life experiences, upon which we can draw for our advantage. So let's talk a bit about experiences and how we can learn more about ourselves from them. As coaches we find clients can easily recount experiences—whether good or not so good, yet they find difficulty linking the quality of the experience with their values.

Your particular set of values has been with you most of your life, although it may not be in the forefront of your mind—and you need to know there isn't a "good" set or a "bad" set. There is a tendency to believe that what life has thrown at us molds who we become. We contend that it's how *we see* what life has thrown at us that molds who we become. It has more to do with our attitude toward the circumstances of our lives...as the saying goes: "Change your attitude—change your life!"

For instance, if we perceive an experience to have been negative—perhaps a particularly sticky divorce, or the early loss of a job—then we shall carry the negative load on our shoulders and it will affect how we see the rest of our life. We fall into the rut of struggling with life, not flowing with it. However, if we decide to think about the good of the experience and ask, "In what way has this been a gift?" we can see the learning we got from it. With this attitude we can begin to move on in our life with loads of positive learning—even if the learning is never to think I've got a job for life again! Here we welcome ease and flow into our lives and diminish the struggle.

Bringing this experience of seeing the rocky patches of our life as positive learning has a huge impact on those around us, especially when the younger people in our circle are going through a tricky time. How good are you at holding the boat steady while someone who is dear to you is getting tossed by the metaphorical storm? Most times they don't need us to solve their problem, they just need to know we are there, having more than survived similar tricky times.

Pulling the positive out from our experiences shifts us into a state of acceptance, wherein lies the greatest potential for serenity and a peaceful mind. However, to move into living with a peaceful mind we need to know what it feels like to have one.

EXERCISE: Digging for Values

Refer back to the timeline you created earlier in the book—would you like to add any other peaks?

Revisit each peak and get in touch with how you were feeling at the time.

Take yourself back to each occasion in turn. Sense the atmosphere, the emotions that were running through you, and the thoughts you were having. Notice what happens in your body when you do this.

Ask yourself what created these feelings. Are there any common threads? These threads are your values. For instance, is there a thread of "freedom to be me, freedom to be you," of "joy of relationship," of "recognition," of "integrity," of "variety and spontaneity," of "jigsaw," of "endless possibilities"? There is no list—use words that come to you. As you find them, put them in your journal. Working through this process you will find that you have a whole range of values, some of which may be contradictory. Know that that's OK too—there is no need to rationalize them.

The purpose of this is not to regress or regret the passing of the years—it's not worth wasting our precious energy. It's to find that we can still recapture the feelings we had at the peak of our performance or experience—and this might mean when we were just sitting on a mountaintop gazing at the view. We don't physically have to repeat the experience or return to that mountaintop to access those feelings in the present. That's what it means to have a quiet mind—when all thoughts move into the background and we feel untouchable, invincible—and so get in touch with our values.

Rosie is one of our clients who actually has as one of her values "swinging through the range." In other words, she thrives on living a full range of different experiences. One minute she can be in an art gallery drinking in the wonders of a masterpiece and the next minute she's lying flat on her back looking up at the ceiling in the Sistine Chapel, or having a good time on the fairground rides with the young people in her life, or just buying fun and tacky merchandise.

Another form of her "swing" is the desire for lots of company at one end and an essential need for having her own space for reflection and calm at the other end.

Rosie has recently been redesigning her life. Knowing that this is one of her core values has helped her incorporate the possibility for all these ranges. Consequently Rosie has lost her self-description of "Aren't I strange?" and moved into "I just love wanting and creating this range in my life." That's what we call taking a new perspective and aligning with her core value!

Another great way of discovering your values is to think about what angers, annoys, or frustrates you. These emotions are triggered by values *not* being honored or aligned. So here you are looking for what is *missing* to have you feel good. Very often this process gets you to the bigger, more generic values that we usually think of such as "'fairness and justice," "individuality," and "selflessness." It allows you to look more closely at what exactly these words mean for you by putting a string of other words with them—words that more clearly define the values for you.

Julie:

When I was approaching fifty years of age, it became clear that I was not honoring some of the values dearest to me: authenticity, individuality, and integrity. I was continually selling out on myself. I had been trying to accept and be OK with certain behaviors that others accepted, even though I really didn't. I let myself get stuck in attending events and activities that *others* deemed important and exciting. My thinking was that if it's OK with so and so, if everyone else thinks this is the "in" thing to do, well, I must be making too much of this. Even though I took this approach, I never had a sense of calm about it.

I attended a workshop in which the leader emphasized how important it was to seek like-minded people so that we could become more of who we are. It made sense to me so I started to do just that through other workshops and events that were based in spirituality. I also began to attend the church where Marianne Williamson was the minister. In no time I noticed there were many people who had similar values to mine, and they weren't the people I worked with or my current circle of friends. I was so relieved to see I didn't have to try to be like others. I didn't have to enjoy going to a hockey game just because everyone else I worked with did. It was OK to be me and enjoy what mattered most to me. My values were of the utmost importance and if I didn't honor them I would become miserable and never be fulfilled.

Getting in touch with your values is crucially important. They are your checklist for rich living in your daily life. As a rule of thumb, if you are feeling good about yourself, your values are being honored; if you feel bad or uncomfortable about something, then it's likely that one or more of your values are not being honored and you need to investigate before any action is taken.

So, what's the point of this? Knowing your values has many uses:

- It helps you understand your reaction to a situation and let go of your attachment to it.
- It helps you value your life experiences in a way that brings your learning to your life now.
- It helps you appreciate that other people have different values and that's why they are different—not worse or better—and this

helps you understand where they are coming from and stops you from getting embroiled in their story.

- It helps you see what is affecting another person and you can then help them get their own concern into perspective.
- Your values give you portals or access points to tap into the vast array of different energies that are available to you.

CHAPTER FIFTEEN

How to "Tap Into"

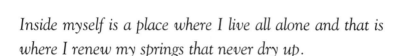

Inside myself is a place where I live all alone and that is where I renew my springs that never dry up.

—Pearl S. Buck

It's interesting that we have chosen the words "tap into" rather than "acquire" or even "access." Knowing that you own and have access to all these powerful energies is one thing—tapping into them so that they serve you in your world is another ball game. The energies are already present in you, rather like a huge reservoir or series of reservoirs. And "reservoir" is a wonderful metaphor to play with. Reservoirs, just like our energies, can get overused with the result that they need replenishing. On the other hand, if they are not drained, they are not being used—and they are certainly there to be used otherwise they fall into neglect. So there is a cycle of draining and replenishing that needs to take place. Knowing whether you are taking from or putting into your particular supply is a way of managing your reservoirs of energy and this management requires conscious effort, conscious choice.

This puts a whole new meaning on self-management. The term self-management is normally confined to managing your behaviors; however, we are now saying that you need to manage the "whole" of you so that you maintain harmony and alignment. Harmony and alignment help to create the quiet mind we have talked about before and raise your level of consciousness.

This seems a good place to remind you that we are blessed with three givens: mind (our inner wisdom), thought (our intellectual ability to think), and consciousness (our ability to give life to our thoughts and hence the life that is around us). The inner wisdom of your mind knows what is best for you and for all concerned; it knows all. When your mind is quiet, free from the intruding, self-defeating thoughts, your ability to tap into your wisdom will increase and enhance your level of consciousness. This is what happens when we have a peak experience—we are available to see so much more that is going on around us.

The expression "needing to recharge my battery" has something of the connotation we are conveying. We need to fill our various reservoirs, especially when we know they are getting dangerously close to empty. What is burnout other than running on empty in every possible energy reservoir? Conscious awareness of the state of our energy—our reservoirs—is essential.

So how do you tap into these various energies so that you can live your life with greater aliveness and more fulfillment?

Having identified your own energies and what they look like, you then need to be able to know how you want to use them—and how they will be replenished. So you need to find out where you are at this point in time, and then look at where you want to be heading. Once you know that, you can start to manage and use your energetic reserves to great effect.

The place to start is by asking yourself:

- *Who am I? (You might want to answer this by referring back to the exercise you did earlier.) What did that tell you about who you are?*

- *Who am I at my core? (Look at the values you wrote in your journal when you did the exercise in the previous chapter. Now that you have had more time to think, do you want to add more?)*

- *How do I honor my values on a daily basis? (A good indicator here is how much you feel in the flow of life, when you feel good about life.)*

- *Where do I sell out on my values? (Notice where you are most uncomfortable, most displeased, or ill at ease—what value isn't being honored?)*

- *What's the external impact I currently create? How do I think people see me? (Have you had any further thoughts since you filled in the outer layer of the exercise in Section One?)*

- *How do I know I have the impact I think I do? (What are you using as your guide, your standard? What are you reading into how people react to you?)*

- *What's the impact I would like to create? (Here it's a good idea to think back to those special moments when you were really who you wanted to be. What was your essence?)*

- *Which sort of energy have I been most aware of in my life?*

- *Which have I been largely ignoring?*

- *Where do I want to focus more attention right now in regard to these reservoirs of energy?*

- *How do I want to self-manage so that I replenish my reservoirs? What needs to change?*

The next place to look is at any habits, customs, ways of doing things that are getting in the way. What needs to shift? We all create our routines or habits that we never question, just because they seem to work for us. Sometimes the reason for doing things in an habitual way has been lost in the mists of time. There doesn't appear to be any need to question them until we consider making changes in our lives. Now's the time to look!

So, yes, you do need to look again at the habits you are perpetuating—like polishing the silver, putting on makeup before going out of the house, running your meetings in the same way, making the same meals on the same day of each week, going to the same place for your vacations, always wearing the same colors, the same hair-style. These may be perfectly good habits for you…or they may not.

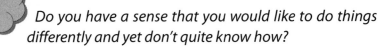

Do you have a sense that you would like to do things differently and yet don't quite know how?

- *Which habits are you using as a crutch, as an excuse not to bring about any changes in your life?*
- *If you were to let go of any particular habits, which would they be?*
- *What would you put in their place?*
- *What new habits might you introduce?*
- *What will help you achieve these changes?*

You could discuss this with a friend and see what comes up. The trick is not to think that there are "good" and "bad" habits—in the same way that there are no "good" or "bad" values. Notice what is important to *you now,* at this point in your life.

The last, but by no means least, area to look at is your dreams. Dreams don't get a very good press these days—they tend to be presented as something pink and fluffy, good for women's magazines or for those interested in the occult. Why do we trivialize dreams when we are the only species on earth that can create and articulate our dreams? Dreams are an expression of our aspirations, our desires; they are not a fantasy. Other than in the career context, our dreams can and do get hugely underplayed. Yet they can be a vital indicator of a need to tap into our energies more deeply or in a different way to move toward fulfilling that dream.

Lynn:

As an educational researcher I did a lot of work with young people in their teens, part of which was asking them about their dreams for themselves. It was sad to hear how many of them thought there was little point in having dreams since "they never come true anyway." I realized that most of these young people were being influenced by the adults with whom they came into contact: parents, grandparents, teachers, and friends, all of whom were imprinting their own feelings on these young people.

Clearly the adults who had influenced these younger people were doing so with good intentions, thinking they knew best yet unaware that they could only see the situation from their own reality, based on their own values and experience. Remember, we can never get into someone else's shoes.

We have proven that dreams can come true because we have fulfilled some of our own dreams over the last few years.

"Dream" is a slippery word and you need to decide for yourself just what it means for you. As we indicated in the first section of this book, to us a dream is anything you want to do at some future time in your life. As coaches we often request that our clients start to design their own lives. This is about getting off the "victim" merry-go-round and getting yourself into the driver's seat. Feel the difference in the sense of the words in these two sentences:

- I would love to climb Mount Everest but I'm too old.
- I would have loved to climb Mount Everest and I know I am too old to start.

The first version holds a sense of regret, blame, victimhood around age. In the second version there is a degree of acceptance that a dream has been lost—it is possible to let it go by recognizing that it is the past, detaching from it, and moving on.

Once we can accept where we are in our journey of life, let go of what has not worked out for us before, or what we have not taken charge of, we can start living from now and designing how we want the rest of our life to be. This, combined with our knowing about our different energies, enables us to put ourselves in the driver's seat because this is the hard truth: "No one else can do it for you; your life is literally in your own hands."

Take a look at the list of things you dreamed of doing from Chapter One. Here's your opportunity to think again, amend them, add to them, and reevaluate—are they authentically you? From where you are right now in your life, are these what you dream of doing before you die?

Dreams feel like a stretch—if they don't you would have done them already. Fantasy, on the other hand, is the unachievable or unassailable. Dreams are definitely within the bounds of possibility yet as we've been saying, your old beliefs may not allow you to readily see the possibility. You will have to be diligent in removing the old "perceived" roadblocks in your mind. *And*, although dreams are within the realm of possibility, boy, will you have to make a bit of effort!

So, knowing who you are and what makes you tick, what habits you want to let go of and what dreams you want to fulfill, you are well set to tap into your own energy reservoirs and "walk through the door" to something new.

Walk Through the Door

*Start the Changes and Shifts
You Want to See in Your Life*

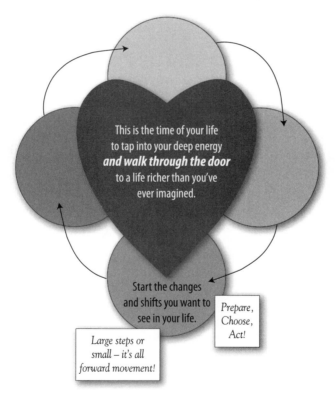

This is the time of your life to tap into your deep energy *and walk through the door* to a life richer than you've ever imagined.

Start the changes and shifts you want to see in your life.

Prepare, Choose, Act!

Large steps or small – it's all forward movement!

Hooray! Here you are entering the third section of the book—the section that gears you up for action! Let's start by exploring further the notion of change and designing our own adventure.

CHAPTER SIXTEEN

Exploring Change— An Adventure

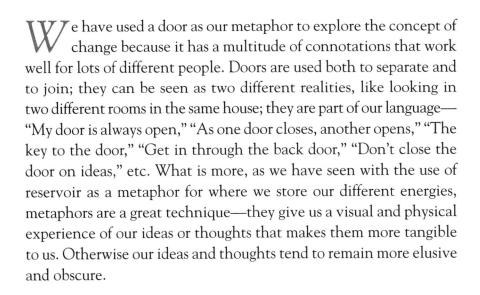

We have used a door as our metaphor to explore the concept of change because it has a multitude of connotations that work well for lots of different people. Doors are used both to separate and to join; they can be seen as two different realities, like looking in two different rooms in the same house; they are part of our language— "My door is always open," "As one door closes, another opens," "The key to the door," "Get in through the back door," "Don't close the door on ideas," etc. What is more, as we have seen with the use of reservoir as a metaphor for where we store our different energies, metaphors are a great technique—they give us a visual and physical experience of our ideas or thoughts that makes them more tangible to us. Otherwise our ideas and thoughts tend to remain more elusive and obscure.

> *I thought how unpleasant it is to be locked out;*
> *And I thought how it is worse, perhaps, to be locked in.*
>
> —Virginia Woolf

When using the door as metaphor, first you need to identify the door, then decide when you will move into action, and finally find a way of actually walking through it if you are to bring about any change you want to see in your life—no matter how great or how small. "Walking through the door" has movement and dynamism in it—it is not a passive door that you can stand and look at for a long time. Certainly you may stand at the door for a bit as you gain clarity on what it represents and what it means for you to walk through it; however, continuing to stand there won't get you through it. To get through the door you must explore how you want to walk through the door—how you will create the changes you want to see in your life that will bring about a transformation for you. In other words, you will no longer be in the room of your life you were in before. You will be moving into a new room and you will want that room to reflect your vision, your dreams, or at least be a room that leads you in the direction you desire. So, you will need to determine the *what*, *when*, and *how* to walk through that door. Only you have those answers and they *are* within you.

First, let's look at *what* it is you want to change. This helps you find the door you want to walk through in the first place. At this point in the book you will have a good idea of who you are and what you bring to your world. You will also have a sense of where the juice is for you. Perhaps you just need to squeeze that aspect a little more? If you are in this place, then your door may be your answer to the following questions:

- What needs to be different in order for you to be able to squeeze a little more?

- What will bring you the added excitement or satisfaction—that juice we speak of?

On the other hand, you may have realized exactly what needs to shift, that some sort of big change is needed—perhaps you need to practice saying no more often in order to reduce that feeling of overload or "got to." Or do you want to take up that interest or activity you've been promising yourself for years? Maybe you want to just get off your butt more—or even sit on it more! There are no rules here as to what the change ought to look like. Only you are privy to that information—it's what will make the difference in your life—no one else's. If when you read that last sentence a little voice came into your head saying, "Of course it will make a difference to others," you are of course right.

We've talked about it earlier—your actions may very well make a difference in someone else's life yet being true to yourself is first and foremost, *and* the difference you create in your relationship may very well be a positive one. For any change there are actions and reactions—in other words, consequences. These are neither good, nor bad—they just are. It's how you choose to see them and deal with them that consigns them to the good or the bad category. You need to remember this when you evaluate the possible consequences of your choices.

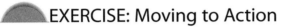EXERCISE: Moving to Action

What is the change you want to focus on?

Refer back to previous exercises about your dreams or new activities to help you choose your change. Having something concrete to work on will make this section real for you. Fully articulate the change by describing it in detail in your journal.

CHAPTER SEVENTEEN

Status Quo— Change Perspectives

*T*here is another way of bringing about change that is impercep-
tible in action, at least at the start, but is highly perceptible in
attitude. Here we are talking about changing the way we see things—
having another perspective on life, on the world. The concept of
perspectives or viewpoints has been introduced at various points
throughout the book and you are probably already challenging some
of your strongly held perspectives.

Many of us get stuck in seeing things only one way based on the
frame of reference we have established throughout our lives—the
thoughts that are ingrained in us. Yet it is a fact that we actually can
choose our own thoughts. Surprising? Not really, but we do not usually actively practice choosing what we think about something or
someone—or even about our own lives. We fall into that autopilot
thought process we've lived with all our lives, never even thinking
we could challenge it.

We only need to look at different cultures to see how they have
different perspectives about what are natural parts of life…and death.
In multiracial communities this level of understanding is paramount
if there is to be peaceful existence. It is not about being right—just
another perspective. Here is a short story that illustrates this point.

In his book *Shaman, Healer, Sage: How to Heal Yourself and Others with the Energy Medicine of the Americas*, Alberto Villoldo, Ph.D., recounts an experience of his that is a moving example of how our viewpoint affects our life. We have shortened and paraphrased his story for our purposes here.

Dr. Villoldo and others were escorting an Indian woman and her sick infant through the Andes Mountains in Peru to get to a clinic. Suddenly the weather became treacherous. The heavy snow and bitter cold forced them to stop and take refuge. Although everything was done to keep the baby warm and protected, she died. The baby's mother was in tears and mourned the loss of her child, yet within a couple of days she was back to her normal activities. Dr. Villoldo instead continued to feel grief over the baby's death and found that the family of the mother and infant were consoling *him* instead of the other way around. Even though the family was deeply saddened by the baby's death, they were unselfish people who displayed great warmth, compassion, and unconditional love.

The community of Indians living in the Andes Mountains accepts death—in their belief, the baby was returned to her mother (Mother Earth). In Western beliefs it may be said that the baby returned to her creator or God. In any case, these Indians are not in the habit of letting the ups and downs of life define the quality of the rest of their lives. They accept death as part of life…they accept the happy times and the sad times and live life as it is presented to them. With this viewpoint they are able to live their life to the fullest.

It's very much in our language to talk about "positive people," as if they are something different. There are people who would belittle positive thinking as if it is something totally false and made up. Yet, as we have said before, each and every one of us lives in our own reality, the world as we see it—indeed as we choose to see it (though that sense of choice may not always be obvious). And in our case, we may have been looking at it this way for a good number of years!

Let's think about something as innocuous as the weather. There are some people who say, "Hooray, it's raining!" Others take the opposite view, and some are just totally indifferent. Why is this? The fact that it's raining has not changed.

Ponder what we are saying for a few moments. Whichever category you are in (love the rain, hate the rain, don't mind the rain, or it depends on what I'm doing), try shifting your perspective to see it from another viewpoint. Maybe your partner loves the rain and you don't. Perhaps the land and crops are in need of water…would that change your outlook? What's it like to look at the fact that it's raining from a "hooray" perspective?

Having expectations about how something—or someone—is going to turn out is another change resister. We tend to get attached to these expectations, and when they don't turn out as we wanted (or expected), surprise! surprise!—disappointment sets in. However, it's not part of our learning to make the connection between having expectations and the frequency of disappointment when these expectations are not met. We are in fact surrounded by media that tell us what to expect in terms of customer services, in loving relationships, in the quality of our food, and on and on. These are broad stereotypes that fail to incorporate what works for the individual.

Let's bring this a little closer to home. How much of your life is influenced and held back by expectations? What were some of the expectations you had about getting older? You might like to make two lists: one about your expectations of yourself and the second, your expectations of others. So for instance, in the one about expectations of yourself, it might be that you expected nothing to change—or it might be that you expected lots to change, especially physically. On the other hand you might expect people you know to continue to treat you as they always have, or you may have swung to the other end of the scale and had an expectation that they would now treat you with more respect. What happens when these expectations are not fulfilled? There may be a disappointment and a "feel bad" factor.

Life's under no obligation to give us what we expect.

—Margaret Mitchell

What are some of the expectations you have been carrying— maybe even for years? Here are a few examples—you may have others that are completely different. There may be disappointments around how your children have turned out; or you may not have ended up with the ideal place to retire; or how your two families get on together; how your partner responds to your needs as you get older. Now notice how these reactions are totally the product of your thoughts. Expectations are created from thinking about how you'd like something to be.

We sometimes expect the other person to have a crystal ball to know what we expect. We set up something like a test, then get disappointed when they fail the test. What do you imagine that might be about?

EXERCISE: Letting Go of Disappointment

Think of a time when you felt disappointed. Spend a few minutes getting in touch with that feeling and how you came to feel disappointed. What were you hoping for or expecting?

Imagine having no expectation or judgment around the outcome. Yes, of course you will feel resistance to trying to see it in this way and may find your inner voice saying, "Ah yes, but...." It may challenge you to let go of a view you have held. However, it is possible to do it and to own that new view. Persevere until you can see the outcome free from any feeling of disappointment on your part.

We shall soon do a little more on changing perspectives. For the moment it is enough to notice that you have judgment and that you can shift away from it. Here is a story that shows the power perspective has on our experiences.

Gloria is a friend who had never been athletic; she was more "cerebral," as she would say. Well, that changed in her late forties when the status quo of her life was no longer acceptable to her. Along with other major life changes she was making, she decided she wanted to run a marathon. That was a tall order; however, with her new goal in mind she set up a training schedule and trained with conviction. After more than a year, she was fit and ready to enter her first marathon.

When the big day arrived Gloria was fighting a leg injury that had occurred two weeks earlier; she was in pain but thought she would be OK. Within the first mile of the race, her leg was not holding up—the pain was different, more severe, and she was already limping. Still she thought she'd be OK, but by the 10-mile mark she knew she either had to completely settle into the pain and run or quit. What she didn't know at the time is that she sustained a new injury in that first mile, which would have put most people out of the race.

Gloria was preoccupied with thoughts of how hard she had worked toward this day—for her, finishing this race meant more than the race itself. It was symbolic of the new life she had created. She wasn't quitting; even though her performance was nowhere near what she had planned and trained for she was determined to finish. And she did, falling into the waiting arms of her children at the finish line!

So, how did Gloria view the reality of her experience and how her race had ended? Was she delighted to have persevered and completed her first marathon run? Was she regretful that she did not give up and stop running the race and save herself considerable pain? Was she disappointed that she was not able to finish in a position she was capable of?

In fact she was none of these. She was able to stay entirely with what had happened and accept the reality free from expectation of what it might have looked like. The facts were:

- She had trained and completed her first marathon.
- She had sustained an injury that she chose to continue to run on.
- She was in severe pain.

That was enough for her.

If you are wondering where her perspective has taken her in the years since—she is now in her early fifties and has three more marathons under her belt, plus she has added ice climbing and road biking to her activities.

Do you see the major difference Gloria's perspective had on her experience of this event and what she took with her? She let go of expectations and the result was positive even if she was injured. Wow, she finished her first marathon and accepted what came with it! If she had held on to her expectations of herself, Gloria could have been quite miserable and not just from the pain of her injury. She could have had thoughts that go something like: "I messed up and ruined the race" and "I didn't stop and now my injury is more serious." That wasn't the route she chose.

Another set of thoughts are those that put you in a place of judgment of others. Phrases like "I don't like people who…" are a good indicator of this kind of thinking. Often it is the *behavior* that is not liked rather than the person. However, the outcome is negative thoughts. Negative thoughts create negative emotions (anger, sadness, resentment) that are your body's warning system or barometer that balance and harmony are about to shift.

So what happens? How do we get so stuck in the way we see things? How do we get stuck with rigid expectations?

We get into a habit, fueled by our beliefs, experiences, stories that this is the way the world is. Yet, as we have seen, how we choose to view it can be very different, and it genuinely is a choice. You are in charge of your own thoughts, how you choose to see your world. This is not necessarily an easy task when we are truly entrenched in one way of thinking. *And,* it is very possible to alter our perspective with conscious effort. We can both attest to that!

> *If you want your life to be more rewarding, you have to change the way you think.*
>
> —Oprah Winfrey

EXERCISE: Different Ways of Looking at It

An effective exercise is to play with perspectives.

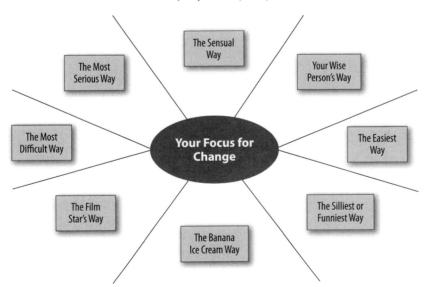

On a sheet of paper, produce your own diagram and in the center write down the change you have chosen to focus on. Now add how you are currently thinking about it. Then ask yourself, "What's a different way of looking at this?" Continue by writing your answers to the

questions around the circle: "What's the most difficult way for me to see this?" "What's the easiest?" "What's the silliest?" and so forth. Take time to consider each perspective in turn—try them on, so to speak. Feel their energy in your body—and notice what resonates with you.

Be in a lighthearted mood and ask your mind (your subconscious actually) to come up with various viewpoints whether or not they make any sense at all—no, really, don't dismiss any of them. In fact this point is key: These perspectives do not all have to make sense—as you will see from some of the viewpoints we've put in the example for you to work on. You may readily uncover a desirable viewpoint or you may find one that is otherwise hidden within a perspective that did not make sense initially.

You will be able to choose new thoughts to replace the old ones that aren't serving you.

What do we mean by "thoughts not serving you"? We are refer-ring to thoughts that take you down the path of victimhood, thoughts such as: "No one's going to support me," "I'm not ready for this yet," "If I had enough money…." Thinking in this manner only hinders you and holds you back.

Consider this perspective: "My change is an adventure."

When you choose new thoughts, your perspective will transform and you'll begin to see that walking through that door of change is indeed an adventure.

> ### Julie:
>
> As I neared the end of my coach training I did a perspec-tives game and looked very closely at my thoughts that held me back from leaving my corporate job. Although I wanted to leave I had several beliefs about why I couldn't. Finally, I chose new thoughts and new perspectives and my eyes opened to the pos-sibilities that had always been there.

I will state the perspectives in terms of what I said yes to and what I said no to. I physically went through the motions and spoke out loud and opened the doors to the yes's and firmly closed the doors to the no's.

I said Yes to:	*I said No to:*
• Being a full-time coach	• My fear of not being good enough
• Having my own office	• Sharing an office with my husband
• Leaving my job	• A regular paycheck and expense account

Even though this was six years ago, I still recall how powerful the physical action of doing this exercise was. My heart was pounding, my body was shaking—and this reaction in my body stayed with me for some considerable time. Making a commitment was real for me. I knew there was no turning back and yet I did not know when I would be able to do it. Well, the "universal phone" rang and I heard it loud and clear. Within one month of doing that exercise, I gave my notice at work—I knew there would never be a better time and I was off on my adventure!

You would never leave for a real adventure without some form of adequate preparation, and bringing about change is the same. It can take just a matter of minutes or months, depending on the nature of the change and, most importantly, your particular way of handling change. What is absolutely certain is there is definitely no need to commit until you are ready to do so. Committing halfheartedly—or even worse, because someone else thinks you should—is a recipe for failure. We assume you want a change where you can close the door firmly behind you rather than fooling yourself by attempting to swing back and forth between the old and the new. That won't work—you are likely to be more unsettled and unfulfilled than ever.

EXERCISE: Adventure Into Change

It's time to see the change you want to make as an adventure.

This is an effective way to let your imagination take you into adventureland! It does not matter what sort of adventure you are imagining—your wisdom will point you to an adventure that is right for you. Let your intuition, your inner voice, take the lead. If negative chatter pops into your mind, recognize it for what it is—a way of distracting you from getting to the possibilities—and the fun too!

Use your journal to describe the nature of your adventure. Think about:

- *What sort of terrain it will take you through*
- *What the climatic conditions are going to be*
- *Who will be there with you—or maybe you will be on your own*
- *What kind of support structure you might need*
- *How you require to prepare for this adventure*
- *Most importantly, who do you need to be during this adventure?*

Describing the details of your adventure will strengthen your resolve. We urge you to use your creativity in making your adventure tangible. For some people it's writing it as a story, for others painting a picture, writing a poem…whatever turns you on—and don't let that "I can't draw/write/paint" gremlin get you!

The objective is to attain a sense of easy flow in life. Life is like a river—it has its slow parts, its rapids, its areas where it gets all churned up, its waterfalls, and yet each of these can be areas of huge natural beauty. *"Life is what happens when you're busy making other plans"* is a well-known quote by John Lennon, the famous Beatle—and we can't stop life happening. The only thing we can do is choose how we want to think about it. And how we think about it defines how we experience it and how we *feel*.

Looking for easy flow is not about looking for an easy life—there's nothing you can do about that. What we are pointing to is seeing how you can make your way with it—really savor the rapids, the slow parts, the waterfalls, the churned up areas, so that it becomes *your* life and you are not just a victim or a bystander.

So here are the choices: you can change your own thinking and/ or you can change your own actions—usually both. Only you can see which door you want to walk through. Only you can choose to walk through it and only you can choose *when* and *how* you are going to walk through it. You might like to consider the quote from Mary Oliver's poem "The Summer Day":

> *Tell me, what is it you plan to do*
> *With your one wild and precious life?*

So, while the *when* truly is in your hands, it's worth bearing in mind that you do only have *one* "wild and precious life." The British author Rose Tremain wrote the simple but deep reminder that:

> *Life is not a dress rehearsal.*

Yes! In their different ways these two women were pointing to the fact that this is it—the live performance! There simply won't be another time. For that reason we say the time is *now*, otherwise the waiting may well get in the way of having the life you genuinely want.

In essence it is all about *choice*—your choice about the *what*, the *when*, and the *how* of your life.

EXERCISE: Toward Commitment

Closing the door behind you is a metaphor for letting go of the past, something that is no longer valid in your life, that no longer serves you. As we have said throughout this book, hanging on to the past hampers us from moving forward; the old patterns leave no space for a new one to form.

- *What habits, what resentments, what old beliefs from your past do you need to release to effect the change you are focusing on? Make a list of them and view them as doors you are closing.*

- *Name each door: "I'm too old," "I'm just a housewife," "What about my pension?" "I've got to put my kids through school," etc.*

- *Draw those doors and visualize closing them, one by one.*

Once you've closed those doors, what are some new doors you'd like to open? Name and draw those too!

- *Practice opening one door at a time and taking a step through the door. Stand up and do this physically to feel it in your body. The physical action brings your experience into the tangible world and is very powerful. Give it a try! Notice how you feel. What impact does it have on you?*

- *You can revisit this exercise anytime to make your commitment to change more tangible.*

It's time to write a Commitment Statement in your journal:

- *What are you leaving behind?*

  I am leaving behind…

- *What are you moving into?*

  I am moving into…

That's great! So when are you going to walk through that door?

CHAPTER EIGHTEEN

Courage—
Standing Up to the Fear

*You gain strength, courage, and confidence by every ex-
perience in which you really stop to look fear in the face.
You must do the thing which you think you cannot do.*

—Eleanor Roosevelt

*What were some of the feelings that came up for you in
the last exercise as you thought about and energetically
practiced going through some doors? What did you feel as you
wrote your commitment? What stops you from going through
a door that heralds a change you have actively chosen? You need to
identify what is stopping you. Fear is usually at the root. Once you know
what it is, you can step around it just like you would an obstacle on
the sidewalk. You get past that obstacle on the sidewalk quite easily,
don't you? Well, the trick is to view the barrier to the door in the same
way you view an obstacle on the sidewalk. If you do so, the barrier
becomes less threatening and it becomes easier to walk through that
door you've chosen.*

Fear can show up in many different guises. Let's look at some of them and how they hold us back: fear of change, fear of the unknown, fear of known past experience, fear of failing, fear of success.

Fear of change: The saying "You can't teach an old dog new tricks" is something we are taught, and some of us live by it almost without questioning. The result of this thinking is the older we get, the more we become convinced that the harder it is to change, so we become fearful of any impending change. Ever hear people saying, "Well, this is the way I've always been"? So if we take on this false belief that it is harder to change as we get older, we slip back into our comfort zone of familiarity or worse yet we never even venture out of that comfort zone of familiarity. We are here to tell you, "That isn't so!" We've both made more dramatic changes in our mature years than we did in our younger years. When we were younger we were too unaware!

Fear of the unknown: We have a natural tendency to avoid what is unknown and unfamiliar to us. And here's what's strange—none of us can possibly know what's in the next second or minute for us. In reality, living in the unknown is totally familiar yet we make up stories in our heads around the possibilities of what might happen just to avoid living with "not knowing," and this makes us feel more comfortable.

For some, avoidance of the unknown is so strong that even painful but familiar habits or beliefs are preferable to stepping up to experience the new but unknown. Do you know of anyone who has put off, say, having an operation because of what they fear might happen, and have preferred to stay with the pain or discomfort; or someone who has stayed in the same job for years and years because they feared putting themselves to the test just in case they failed to be offered another job? Have you ever had a similar experience? If so, then fear of the unknown, not *you*, was in *your* driver's seat.

Fear of past experience: One of the ways we use to avoid the "not knowing" is to rely on past experiences. They can be real allies or hidden enemies. What has happened in our past does influence how we see things in the future. Here again, conscious choice is where we must place our attention.

Here are a couple of examples of what we mean.

Some of you may be approaching the end of paid employment, or collecting a pension. Inevitably this brings with it your own past experiences, perhaps of your parents, grandparents, aunts, and uncles reaching this same point in their lives. If theirs was a good experience you are likely to see your upcoming experience more positively; the reverse is also true.

Perhaps you've had a car accident on the freeway and now no longer drive on the freeway. Put yourself, not your fear, back in the driver's seat!

Seeing your own or others' past experience as transferable is to fail to realize that the context, the circumstances, and the individuals involved are all very different. What is important for you is that your choice to change is free of self-limiting beliefs, free of hanging on to past experiences, free of clinging to stories that no longer serve.

Fear of failure: A big story we hang on to is failure—we want to avoid it, we fear it, because we link together "failing at something" and "being a failure" as though they were one and the same thing—and of course they are not. This is a huge fear for many of us and is often founded on past beliefs and experiences from our early days—disappointing our parents, letting ourselves down, losing out because we weren't chosen for something we wanted to do. We can easily sink into the "better not to do it at all than fail" way of being. Our society does not like people who make mistakes; no one should make them. Oh no, we must be right and be successful, no mistakes, uh-uh. Does that ring a bell for you?

> *If you have made mistakes, even serious ones, there is always another chance for you. What we call failure is not the falling down but the staying down.*
>
> —Mary Pickford

Have you ever thought about the people who make the most mistakes? Generally speaking, they are the ones who are the most successful. Many successful business owners have made mistake after mistake to get to where they are now. Think of all the "failures" inventors have made…they all eliminate what doesn't work and continue to find what does. So when you make a mistake or an apparently wrong choice, it might not feel good at the time. It's OK to "be" with the feeling of failure for a while. Then let your natural resilience come into play and you'll find yourself bouncing right back up there ready to try another way of reaching your particular goal.

We may encounter many defeats but we must not be defeated.

—Maya Angelou

Fear of success: How about that one! This fear is more common than most of us would expect—don't we all want to be successful? Hmmm, and yet this fear is a major one for many of us. It may be hidden from your consciousness, so take a long look at what is going on; notice if you have negative thoughts about success. They may not be obvious at first so pay attention to even the slightest concern.

Louise had started a small business, and through coaching it was uncovered that she feared success. This is what was holding her back, not fear of failure—no, her barrier was the fear of success. She was afraid her life would change too much: If her business took off, what would happen to the free time she enjoyed? Would she become a slave to her business? She was not willing to give up the freedom she had become accustomed to. In time the "aha" moment finally came—she realized that she would always have a choice as to how much business she did or didn't want to take on. That she *always* had the choice and could make different choices again and again. This insight was such a relief to her…she didn't have to choose one lifestyle over another. She could design her life the way she wanted, keep her business at the level she desired, and have the free time she found so valuable. This freed her to pursue her business with much joy and enthusiasm.

As you contemplate the possibility of successfully achieving your change, are you sitting with fears of losing some of your freedom or certain aspects of your lifestyle you cherish? Are you running the story in your imagination that it will require too much of your time, time you don't want to invest? Are you wondering what will happen to your relationships? Will your friends still be your friends? Will you see your family as often as you like? How will your spouse or partner feel about your being successful? How much will your life change—will it change in ways you like or dislike?

Remember, you always have a choice at every single stage of your journey. So if great success does come your way, you can choose how much you want and how much you want to pass up. Think of it, great success may increase your finances, and that would put you in a position to hire out certain tasks that you currently do yourself. Let's repeat again: You are in the driver's seat. There's no need to be bowled over—even by your own success. You can spend your time doing what you do best—what fulfills and satisfies you.

Our deepest fear is not that we are inadequate;
our deepest fear is that we are powerful beyond measure.
It is our light, not our darkness that most frightens us.

—Marianne Williamson

EXERCISE: Facts and Fiction

Please do not just glance over the questions in this exercise. Your answers will help you move your change forward. Listening to your inner wisdom will be enlightening if you simply allow. Ponder these questions when your mind is quiet, possibly in that deeper meditative place we have suggested in other exercises.

As you think about the changes you have been working on:

- *What fears come up for you?*

- *What happens when you face them head-on?*

- *What thoughts are creating your fear?*

- *How valid are these thoughts? Distinguish the facts from the fiction.*

Drop the fiction that you've identified! Look at the facts and choose thoughts that empower you rather than disable you.

It is normal to feel fear and to have resistance; it is absolutely natural and not to be taken as a sign that you are making a mistake. Unless, of course, you have not already done the serious introspection we've been talking about. Doing your inner work is crucial. *And*, if you do end up making a mistake, it's not the end of the world; it is there to show and teach you something. It does *not* make you a failure. Only you and how you think about yourself can do that.

In either case, when the fears and resistance pull at you, there is a need for acknowledgment and gentleness. If a child had the same fears and you were to support this child, what would you say to her? Remind yourself of your wisdom, your intelligence, your creativity, your inner beauty…you are all of these things and many, many, many more!

EXERCISE: Managing the Emotional Barometer

Let's take a look at a possible scenario to show how fear is the emotion emanating from a large number of thoughts that we are usually barely aware of.

Let's imagine the change you want to see is to take up a lifelong yearning to do something—we know a lot of women who long to play a musical instrument, for example. Yet there is a feeling of fear. What is it about? Example: Fear that I won't be successful. It's silly to think I can do this now.

Ask yourself the following questions:

- *What does successful look like to you?*
- *Can success look another way?*
- *Who are you comparing yourself to?*
- *What will happen if you are not successful?*
- *Is this really true?*
- *What are your expectations of yourself?*
- *What would it be like to let go of the expectations?*
- *What if this change were simply an adventure?*
- *What if your focus was not the end result but the process of playing the instrument?*
- *What enjoyment might you gain from finally allowing yourself to play the instrument?*

Take one of those ten dreams you wrote down earlier—perhaps one you've not worked with and around which you have a feeling of fear. Now try working with the root of your fear in a similar way.

Remember, you are the designer of your choices. There isn't a "right" and a "wrong," simply a choice that works for you. What won't work is if you choose to sell yourself short and not go through your chosen door. You chose the door—no one else. So if you decide to back out, what is that about? Perhaps it's mind chatter creating more resistance. Even if you don't walk through your chosen door, what fears do you still have on this side of the door? Explore them in more depth. It could be that this *isn't* the door for you or at least not at *this* time. Tap into your inner wisdom; the answer is there.

Someone once described fear as being like elastic strings attached to you. The harder you pull away, the more fear and resistance you feel. Those elastic strings pull back with greater force as you pull away. So what's the trick? There isn't a way of getting rid of fear, so there is no point in waiting for the fear to go away. Look at the validity of the fears that are coming up for you. One way of doing this is by asking yourself: "What's the worst thing that could happen?" followed by "So what?" This "So what?" is not intended as an offensive question. Asking "So what?" can bring the truth to the surface—the truth that the world won't come to an end, that your life will not be ruined, that for the most part, your fear is largely unfounded.

Fear is often referred to as an acronym with different meanings. The best known is that FEAR stands for "False Evidence Appearing Real." How does that sit with you?

When you decide to walk through that door, the best thing you can do is trust. Trust knowing that:

- Your natural resilience will be there to keep you afloat.
- Your ability to change your perspectives will serve you in any given moment.
- You are free in every second of your life to make a choice—the chosen path can have as many twists and turns as you choose.
- There will always be consequences to the choices you make—you just have to learn to dance with them.
- There is no cheese at the end of the tunnel if you cling to expectations. (Read *Who Moved My Cheese?* by Spencer Johnson and Kenneth H. Blanchard.)

As author Susan Jeffers says, *Feel the Fear and Do It Anyway*. That is what is often required when stepping out of the old way. Feeling your knees or hands shaking and still taking that step forward takes courage and faith. Bottom line, is your dream or intention to have a richer life worth the dry mouth and pounding heart when you reach a crucial juncture? Does what you desire mean enough to you to walk through the fear? You will have to decide what is more important, avoiding the fear or following through with your dream. Will you be at peace with yourself if you avoid the fear and let go of your dream?

And because the fear feeling never goes away—it is closely allied to high excitement—do not forget that courage is needed to continue on your journey with fear by your side. This is why it is so very important to know exactly what change you want to see in your life. The stronger your desire, the stronger will be your courage.

When we met Betty she was nearing the age of fifty and was suffering from rheumatoid arthritis (RA). Her former career was in dance and the adjustment to living with RA was hitting hard. For the previous eighteen years she had proceeded through various stages of the condition and the telltale signs of RA disfigured her hands. We were in the same training course, and she told us right from the beginning that she smoked weed because it helped her pain. She did not want us to think badly of her—she had carried this secret around for six years never having shared it with others, so it took a great deal of courage for her to tell us, a group of twenty-six people whom she barely knew.

We were in a ten-month course involving four one-week retreats. By the end of the first retreat she had already decided she could give up the weed and let her mind and intuition control the pain.

As we moved through the program she progressively chose to demand more and more of herself, pushing through the fear of greater pain in the full knowledge that if and when it came she would find a way of handling it better.

By the end of the program she was on simple medication, vastly reduced from what it was originally, and she was designing and delivering classes to help people see how they can have a voice as a patient to be able to express what they want for their bodies, just as she had done.

Remarkably, some three years later she is able to dance sufficiently to train others and pass on her beautiful art. All this plus another more recent change—she no longer takes any medication whatsoever! She is practicing self-healing and the illness has significantly regressed.

How is that for having the commitment and courage? Don't think that it was all a breeze for Betty—no, not by a long shot. She had quite a few doors to walk through, yet it is all worth it because now she is living the fuller, richer life she wanted and deserved.

One of the things we have learned over the years of coaching many women approaching the second half of their lives is that sometimes we have to do some cycling around until we get to the point where it feels right to walk through that door. It's entirely one thing knowing that you want some sort of change and quite another actually stepping into that change by walking through the door. That takes courage—lots of it—and sometimes that courage, rather like a muscle, has to be built up until it is ready to take the strain. Even small changes can require courage, so start with those just like you would gradually start with muscle strengthening exercises.

When beginning a work-out regimen we do not jump in with the most aggressive routine because if we do, we either injure ourselves or become so sore, we cannot continue. Instead we work our way up to it. It is the same with these changes—work your way up to the big ones, strengthening your courage muscle as you go, and the experiences will make subsequent changes less of a struggle, with more and more possibilities opening up for you. At some point, it will feel quite the norm to feel fear, just like a routine exercise you've been at for months and months.

Life shrinks or expands in proportion to one's courage.

—Anaïs Nin

Sue loves horses but had a very bad experience when she was younger, which brought up lots of fear about going near horses for the rest of her life. She had rationalized that her fear and inability to ever own or ride a horse again was because of her highly pressurized job; because she was out of practice; didn't have a regular schedule so couldn't go regularly; couldn't possibly own a horse again until she had the right sort of house, land, etc.

Sue had never brought this issue to any of her coaching calls—there were always more pressing issues. However at an intuitive level she knew it was something that absolutely had to change. A couple of times she committed to taking riding lessons—and a couple of times she did not fulfill her commitment...and still the whole issue did not go away. She would find herself drawn to riding stables on her drive home or seek out information about classes on horse management.

Eventually she found what she was looking for—a seminar with the famous "horse whisperer," an open opportunity to go along with a friend to see what this man could do with horses manifesting behavioral difficulties. This was the threshold, the start that she needed.

Over a period of months Sue attended one of this man's courses and discovered lots about herself; she plucked up the courage to take some riding lessons. This was followed by a course on horse ownership, which opened the way to taking a different perspective on what was possible for her in terms of looking after a horse even while she was still in her high-pressure job.

So here she was: livery stable all lined up and now looking for a horse, trusting absolutely that the right horse would find her. It took a while, a lot of perseverance, and a never-failing trust in her intuition that she'd know when the right horse came along—and he did.

What is of note here is that none of this was planned. Her desire was so strong that the universe had her cycle round and round, getting nearer and nearer to fulfilling her desire—almost without her realizing.

Of course, there are times we can fool ourselves. We admire someone who moves forth into areas we are fearful of and we tell ourselves "She's fearless" or "I can't do that because I'm too afraid." This is an easy way out—the negative feedback in our mind is sabotaging us. The truth is that people do move forward in spite of their fears. They will however have built up their courage muscle sufficiently to support them through the fear so that they not only survive but thrive. They also recognize their yearning, their urge must be followed if they are to thrive. Have you ever heard of long-time celebrities who continue to be filled with fear when approaching a performance…yet it doesn't stop them? In fact many of them actively seek more and more demanding roles because they know at their core there's much more potential in them and they can override their fear.

When we talk about courage and strength, we must realize that those characteristics do not exist if there is no fear. If you are not afraid of something, then you do not need to be courageous or strong. This is worth repeating: If there is no fear, there is no courage; courage is needed when there is fear. So, how willing are you to test your courage and strength?

Don't be dismayed with yourself if you have found yourself moving away from an identified change, labeling it as "nonsense" and "impossible" and turning back to what you think is your status quo.

The hard truth is that you are not back—and cannot go back—to your status quo. You have already moved on and started to build your courage muscle. Be kind and gentle with yourself while continuing to move ahead in your own way and in your own time. Also know that by some strange quirk, if you are refusing to pick up the "universal telephone" of change right now, it will start to ring again, and again, until you are in a place to pick it up. The universe is very helpful like that. You will continue to get messages, feel the inner yearning if it is truly something that is to be. *It is never too late.*

It's never too late to be what you might have been.

—George Eliot

CHAPTER NINETEEN

Endless Possibilities— *You Are the Only Limit!*

We guess it's already pretty clear there is not just one possible path in your life and there are many, many possibilities to choose from, many, many doors you could choose to walk through. You can step into being the designer of your life, working with the values you hold, reducing the fears and self-limiting beliefs you may carry, and having a strong sense of what would give you a more fulfilled and balanced life.

> Julia knew she had to make a change in her life; she was reaching burnout, was in permanent pain because of rheumatism and needed a hip replacement. Yet she felt she could not make this decision because she was the only breadwinner in her family.
>
> A short period of coaching brought her to realize that she simply had to make a choice—and that it was indeed a choice she could make. She knew there would be consequences, most of which hovered around having less money. A shift in her perspective allowed her to see there could be a whole host of other consequences she could not possibly even conceive of from

where she was. A shift needed to happen before she could get a better view over the parapet of possibilities.

If you could see her now you would not recognize her as being the same person. She left her job, had her hip surgery, took on some consultancy work, and has had more holidays and time with her husband than she has had in years. Her self-confidence has gone through the roof too.

So it's time to turn up the volume a little bit more.

A truly satisfying and rich life doesn't just happen on its own. You must revisit those aspects we have talked about over and over again throughout life. Check in with yourself regularly by asking yourself questions, such as:

- *In what way am I honoring my values on a daily basis?*
- *How well am I doing in fulfilling my dreams and desires?*
- *How far have I progressed in building my courage muscle, reducing fears and self-limiting beliefs?*
- *How am I choosing to see my life as it is right now?*
- *What do I need to let go of if I don't like the perspective I am in?*
- *How open am I to all the possibilities? What limiting thoughts are getting in my way?*
- *What does the balance I want to see in my life look like right now?*

We are presenting you with this opportunity to look at what is possible for you *now* in your life. How much of your old thinking can you actually throw away in order to make space for some new stuff? Again, if need be, start with something small.

Guided meditations are a great tool to tap into our subconscious to see what we know and want deep down. What we are seeking is the essence, rather than the action. The following is a guided meditation to help you connect with your essence—it resides in you right now. Our subconscious is a treasure trove of who we are at our core. It is the place where we know the essence of who we truly are…tap into it!

EXERCISE: Guided Meditation to Your Essence

Find a space and time for yourself when you will not be disturbed. You can choose to record this guided meditation—or you can read it and remember it so that as you relax you will recall and visualize what is said.

Start by taking three or four deep breaths and close your eyes. Become aware of your body from the top of your head to your toes. Relax and feel heavy. Take plenty of time here to get fully relaxed. Feel how comfortable you are and imagine you are on a small boat with lots of cushions where you can lie down and enjoy the journey. The boat is going to take you along the River of Your Life to meet the "real" you in all your glory with no encumbrances.

As you get comfortable, feel the boat gradually drift out into the river and let it carry you along. You don't have to steer—you can spend the time looking up at the beauty of the sky; feel the air wafting over your face; smell the freshness of the air around you, listen to the sounds of the birds or the water lapping gently on the side of the boat. Just relax; keep breathing deeply as the boat takes you along. As you pass through the twists and turns of this river, feel your cares and personal "baggage" drifting away from you, making you lighter and happier. You are so comfortable and relaxed. Notice all that you see and feel.

'Round the next bend is an area where the boat will land. Imagine this to be a place that is most special to you—a place that exists or one that you have made up in your mind. There could be lush greenery, a waterfall, a meadow, a mountain—any setting that suits you best in this moment. When the boat settles in, disembark and spend some time soaking in this environment. Find a spot to sit—it can be

something in nature, a luxurious lounge chair if that is your prefer-ence, or anything at all. Just let your imagination flow.

Again, while sitting take notice of what is so desirable to you about this place. It is significant since you chose it. In a few moments you will be approached by a woman who is the essence of you. As you are be-ing approached, what do you sense about her? How does she approach you? How does she move? Does she speak to you or do you speak first? You are meeting the core of "you." You are happy to be in each other's company. Remain observant about how she looks—even how she feels to touch, how she smells.

You have the opportunity to ask her what message she has for you. Listen carefully to the answer. It may come in the form of words, body movement, or some particular action. Feel yourself fully alert to what is happening. [Pause]

Now you can ask her any other questions you want. For instance, you might want to ask her how to access your courage; or what your next step will be; or what the key to getting the rich life you want is. Again, listen very carefully to what she tells you. [Pause]

Thank your essence for coming to you and sharing her wisdom with you. As she is ready to leave ask her: "What will help me access you in the future?" Listen very closely. Then allow her to fade away knowing that you will remember all that you are meant to. She is no more than a thought away from you.

It is time to return to the boat that will take you in comfort along the River of Your Life knowing you will feel wiser and stronger. Get your-self comfortable in the boat; reflect on the meeting you have just had and let the river take your boat as you relax. Feel the bobbing of the boat as it moves back along the river. As the boat brings you into land, stay silent for a few moments and when you are ready, open your eyes and jot down what you recall of your experience. Do not force your thinking—just let the words drift from your pen onto the paper. Know that all you remember of what you heard, saw, sensed, and imagined will be significant in helping you achieve the shift in your life.

As you reflect on what you have remembered, look for the threads and links to your values, your beliefs, and the dreams that you have already unearthed. Your subconscious will have prioritized what is most significant for you as you move forward in life.

Find an object or symbol to remind you of how you can access your essence in the future. If it was a word, write it down. Put your reminder where you will see it daily.

As you read through this exercise you may have found yourself resisting leaving the outer coating of your life behind. That is perfectly natural. Know, however, that when you approach the exercise in a relaxed state as a guided meditation, it will leave you easily and provide you with a wealth of information that will resonate deep in your heart. We are all on our life's journey and the more we are in our essence when taking the journey, the richer it will be.

One of our clients is an artist and a teacher. Diane has been teaching for a good many years and has recently come to terms with the fact that she is denying her more creative side. She thought she had rationalized why this had to be the case—she is a single parent with dependent teenagers; she needs a reliable salary; she should be presenting a stable environment for her children's development. All the sort of stuff we tell ourselves when we just *know* there's a change looming.

Regardless of this rationalization, the fact that she was denying one of her core values was not giving her a fulfilling life despite meeting all her self-created criteria. These latter were very much in the list of "should do" rather than "want to." It was having an impact.

She undertook a guided meditation where she found herself in her own studio, surrounded by her own work. Diane saw herself as settled, happy, fulfilled. She sensed there was not huge wealth around her; she saw that she was the creator of the artwork she could see; she had a clear sense of what else there was in her life.

Just by undertaking this simple, non-predictive exercise she was able to free herself from the "shoulds" and open herself to other possibilities.

The upshot is that she has as an intention to create her own studio at some future point and she is starting her journey toward that. However, a more immediate result is that she realized she could create her own studio space in the corner of her own living room right *now*; that she could be responsible for instigating more creative-type conversations in her workplace. In other words she was able to take responsibility *both* for the *now* of her being *and* for her future intention.

After you've done the guided meditation and have a real sense of your essence and what you want your change to look like, it's also effective to articulate your commitment. You can do this as part of your visualization. It gives you the opportunity to "feel" the commitment you are making. Then it will help if you put it out "live." You've already written a Commitment Statement. Now we're talking about actually telling someone.

Who can you tell? Who will hear your intention without being judgmental or trying to persuade you not to do it, or giving you further advice or guidance? Finding this person can be a challenging task—it is usual for others listening to you to want to contribute by giving their view on what you are saying, trying to protect you or help you see the logic of the situation, at least from their perspective. You may have to request the person with whom you are going to share your intention to merely listen to your commitment to your chosen change without comment, whether in favor or against.

Describe where you are heading, when you intend to start your change, and what the purpose of your change is. Promising to provide this person with a follow-up on your progress is a way to hold yourself accountable. You have now shared your intention with someone else—what's going to help keep you on track, keep moving forward? Notice we are pointing here to your intentionality—it is a map in the making, not a rigid one to follow. Any of you who have ever been to one of the weight-loss clubs will know how they make it work—they use allies…the "we're all in it together, girls" type of allies.

In your journey you will benefit from allies. Going it alone is not a great idea. Who might you have for your allies? Allies come in a whole range of categories—you can have an ally who is going to cheer you along and keep you going; another may be a co-worker, someone who is walking a similar path; another may be your champion—they are going to tell others about the great things you are doing. Another may be your resource person—the one who knows where to get whatever it is you need in the moment; even the person who thinks you can't do it can be your ally as she or he is the one who inadvertently will encourage you the most!

EXERCISE: Building Allies

Think about the change you want to make and, at the same time, about the people you know—or may need to get to know—in order to make this intention a reality for you.

- *Who is the person who will come and get you when you start to flag or have self-doubt?*
- *Who is the person with the best contacts for what you need?*
- *Who will keep cheering you along and really believe in you?*
- *Who is the person who falls into the "we're all in it together" category?*

Now that you've identified your allies it's time to start talking to them. When will you do this? Pick up the phone and set a schedule in your calendar.

———————————————

When you look starkly at change it's daunting. Now we've helped you find the rich wealth of resources available to you: your allies, your values, your essence and passions, your courage, your new perspectives, your freedom to choose, and your release from self-limiting beliefs—look how many possibilities there are and how easy it can be to create change in your life.

Carole is one of the people who helped give us the realization of the importance of savoring and we are grateful to her for that. Carole, like us, had trained as a coach and we met in the same leadership program. Here's her story two years later. You will see that it's taken a number of different twists and turns, certainly into places even Carole could not have imagined without allowing for those possibilities just to happen. Nevertheless she has held her intention of making life richer, "tastier" through savoring and, at the same time, has been prepared to show who she is and listen to her intuition to show her what's next. We could say that when friends asked her to do projects it was the universal telephone ringing and pointing her to where she might want to look for more juice in her life. As she describes her journey she writes:

Although I have every intention of completing one if not both of the books I have on the go right now, in addition to running my holiday homes rental business, I have always had a passion for "making things more beautiful"—redecorating our Kentucky home as well as our rental homes. Over the years I have been asked by several friends to "help" them with their decorating projects—with satisfying results. I feel I am in my essence when I have a paint brush in my hand or am "fixing up" something I find at a yard sale. For the past two years I have been redecorating our Kentucky home. I began with creating more space in my bedroom (changing from king to queen bed); buying new (inexpensive but special) pieces of furniture; and finally new carpeting. Result—I love the room and feel comfortable in it and even sleep better in it. The "bedroom project" led me to change some of the furniture in our family room. I passed some of the "old" down to our son, who was delighted. I gave the room a totally new look to rid the clutter (baggage) of years past and to reflect the personal changes I have made in recent years and the person I am today. I then had the 15 yr. old wallpaper removed in the entrance/kitchen/ dining room and had a fresh coat of paint put on walls. I find it so freeing to de-clutter all the "stuff" that has grown up around me for many years. I am only putting back things that I love.

All this led me to an awareness of how much I love to decorate and how it's really not a chore for me. I am going to New York City next week to take a week long "USE WHAT YOU HAVE" decorating class and study with Lauri Ward. I have never been to NYC and think it is time for me to go!! I am following my PASSION and I just know that this is the next thing I must do.

What comes up for you when you consider there are possibilities you've not yet imagined? How about possibilities you may never think of? Does this intrigue you? It does intrigue us because we know the possibilities for each and every one of us are endless, they truly are! Think about it—our human mind is limited—we cannot even conceive of all the potential that exists because it is beyond human comprehension. There is, however, no limit to the higher power that is beyond human form—the power that created all that is, that provides the energetic connection we mentioned in earlier chapters. Opening your mind to that is powerful—it opens the doors and acts as the impetus that will have you walking through the door.

I am where I am because I believe in all possibilities.

—Whoopi Goldberg

CHAPTER TWENTY

Why Walk?

The metaphor of the door represents our being able to access something new that will remain unseen until it is opened. In other words there is no way that the change can be experienced until the door is opened and you step into the change. Here we emphasize that you "walk" through the door. Thinking about doing something is nothing more than that and unfortunately so many of us get stuck here…spending a great deal of time and energy stalling and only *thinking* about doing something. Why do we do that? It certainly does not, and cannot, bring about change. Only actions can do that. There is no alternative, you must open the door first and walk through to see and experience what is on other side. Think of it as walking through a door into another room of a magnificent mansion. If you don't like it or don't want to stay in that room, you can choose to leave. There will always be another door, another room for you to enter and explore. To deepen the metaphor a little, you've got to be ready to dance if you're going to choose the ballroom, or be ready for the heat if you're going to cook some new dishes for you to savor in the kitchen. However, regardless of the room you are planning on entering, be sure to close the door firmly behind you!

Why would we have suggested walking through the door, as opposed to running or leaping or even crawling?

Walking is a way of pacing yourself, giving you the opportunity to clearly see all there is on the other side of the door. It's an opportunity to savor the experience of change and notice its impact both on you and on those around you. We don't want you to miss any of this experience by running.

Lynn:

It may surprise you to learn that the idea for this work was spawned in one minute and then developed in five minutes while Julie and I were balancing on a high wire forty feet in the air as part of our leadership program.

I'm choosing to put this story here because it was without doubt one of the longest and yet most memorable six or so minutes of my life. Here I was partnered with Julie who was recovering from a broken foot and me absolutely petrified of heights—despite this being our fourth or fifth exercise up in the air. We were instructed to give a presentation on our chosen subject while climbing up a tree, stepping onto the end of a high wire attached to the tree, balancing on it standing side by side, and moving toward the center of the wire. All we had for balance were ropes dangling vertically above us spaced several feet apart. (No worries, we had all the safety gear—and somehow it didn't make it any less daunting!)

So what do you come up with as a title for a presentation when you are given sixty little seconds? It's amazing how many possibilities you can go through in that time! The winner was "Staying Sexy after 50."

I very generously (or selfishly) offered to let Julie climb up the tree first while I started the presentation; then she took over the presentation as I climbed up, foothold by foothold on toward the wire until I could finally haul myself up and grab the first rope. It was like everything was happening in slow motion—there was Julie doing her piece, filling the air with her voice; there was my inner critic telling me how dangerous, stupid, silly all this was; there was my person at core saying,

"You're just going to do this no matter what," and below us our audience.

Then something amazing happened—we started to have such fun, rocking backward and forward on this wire, each of us clinging on to a dangling rope and presenting anything at all that came into our heads on our chosen topic. The intuitive radar between us was intense—each sensing what the other had to say, playing with the ideas and comments coming from our audience, loving every moment. We even choreographed our finale—because there's only one way off and that's to jump and be caught by the belay rope—which we succeeded doing in tandem yelling something that probably isn't even printable.

That sure was one heck of a door I walked through and I savored every single moment of it.

Julie:
Yes, that was one heck of a door that I'll always remember with great joy and satisfaction!

In our experience, when we have made changes or when our clients have made changes, the consequences looked nothing like neither we, nor they, had anticipated. Yet that preparation allowed all of us to deal with whatever came up, without running back to the status quo. In other words, once you have decided to walk through your own particular door, close it firmly behind you and stop looking back at it. If you do not close the door you haven't made a clear choice. It's like standing with one leg in one room and the other in another room swaying back and forth…where exactly are you? If you don't know exactly where you are, either forging ahead toward your chosen direction or trying to get back to the status quo—then you will not be in a good position to enjoy the walk.

Now, aged 50, I'm just poised to shoot forth quite free straight and undeflected my bolts whatever they are.

—Virginia Woolf

Regardless of your chosen change, the process of moving into and through change is just as important as achieving the change itself, and you are in charge of the pace and timing of this too. In this respect, therefore, there is no hurry so far as appreciating the process is concerned. In order to do this you need to slow the process right down, rather than jumping from one outcome to another without looking at how you are actually getting to that outcome.

There is in fact huge value in slowing life down so that you can savor your new way of being as it shifts from moment to moment as you experience new relationships and new responses.

And if you are still sitting on the fence, stalling about the *when* and the *how*, it's worth remembering that those seconds you have just enjoyed as you read the previous sentence will never be yours again. Isn't it worth not letting them just slip through your fingers? What a lot of time can be spent waiting for work to end, waiting to get home, waiting to reach a particular birthday, waiting until there is enough money. All this waiting is wishing life away rather than living in the moment, for that is all there is.

It may be that taking this step to slow down and savor the process—even savoring the niceties of everyday life—can constitute a change in its own right. We'll come back to more savoring in the next section.

So here you are, armed with your vision, your courage, your commitment, and your allies. You are ready to walk through the door and start heading toward your chosen change, your richer life—feeling good in mind, body, and spirit. This is essential. Change is no good unless you feel good and excited about it. See it, feel it, embrace it, and rejoice in it!

We are now asking you to go through the door without necessarily being aware of the path. Any journey is full of unknowns, so small goals are essential along the route. Very often we have been taught to plan to the nth degree before doing anything. This usually results in stasis as we spend too much time identifying the dangers, disadvantages, what might go wrong and we get scared. The end result in so many instances is that we just don't follow through, we remain frozen with fears—fears that are not real.

Just know that whatever change you have chosen is founded upon good ground—the good ground of who you are and what will give you greater fulfillment in your life. Think of all the people who followed their dream and then later speak of their amazement at all that transpired; all the magic that entered their life—well beyond their wildest dreams.

I wanted a perfect ending. Now I've learned, the hard way, that some poems don't rhyme, and some stories don't have a clear beginning, middle, and end. Life is about not knowing, having to change, taking the moment and making the best of it without knowing what's going to happen next.

—Gilda Radner

Section Four

A Richer Life

Reflect, Appreciate, and Celebrate!

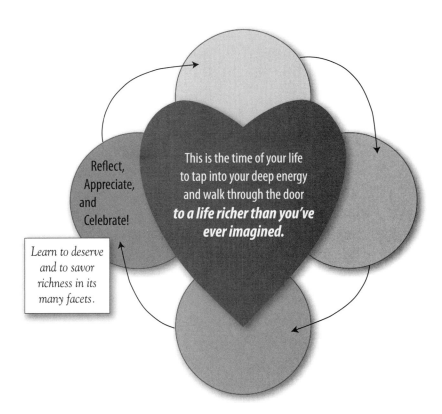

Reflect,
Appreciate,
and
Celebrate!

This is the time of your life
to tap into your deep energy
and walk through the door
*to a life richer than you've
ever imagined.*

*Learn to deserve
and to savor
richness in its
many facets.*

Here we are at the last section of the book, which is juicy since it is all about having a richer life than you've ever imagined.

The objective in this section is to help you determine what a richer life might look like for you and how you can experience it. We have several ideas and viewpoints to share, and it is important for you to keep in mind that the richer life is yours and yours alone to discover and clarify. We are not talking here about being money-rich in the sense of dreaming about winning the lottery, though this does not preclude money-making from being one of the facets of your new, richer life. Absolutely not, you deserve material riches too! Our focus is much more on the "being" of richness than the "doing" and we explore this more in the next chapters.

CHAPTER TWENTY-ONE

What Is Richness?

There is a wide variety of meanings that can be given to the word richness; we use it to describe a feeling or a state of being rather than a doing, as we stated above. It can be a sense of satisfaction, fulfillment, and/or joy. It is the abundance and gratitude you feel within as well as the connectedness you feel to others. Then again, richness is not only what is labeled as "good." It can be felt through a tragedy, a sadness that is accepted and fully experienced.

Richness is being fully present with what *is*—being in the *now* that we have referred to throughout this book—allowing yourself to feel and absorb all that is happening…all that surrounds you. Fully living every minute of your life.

> *I don't want to get to the end of my life and find that I have just lived the length of it. I want to have lived the width of it as well.*
>
> —Diane Ackerman

As humans we have a wide range of emotions and characteristics, and because of our self-judgment (and the perceived or real judgment of others) we often suppress them. We not only want to be seen in a specific way and maintain our self-image, we also want to feel only certain emotions, be it happy, enthusiastic, energetic, and so on. We block out what we view as negative emotions and aspects of our personalities in an attempt to control what we do or do not actually feel, what we do or do not want to deal with. It is only natural that our unconscious mind works to avoid feelings that are undesirable, uncomfortable, and even painful for us—it is trying to protect us. However, the result is that we end up living in a narrow field allowing ourselves only so much sadness and therefore, only so much happiness.

Imagine that your emotions are like a pendulum...the pendulum will only swing as far to one side as it does to the other. When you squelch your sadness, anger, and other "negative" emotions, you limit your ability to experience true joy and aliveness. You limit the "positive" feelings to the extent you feel the negative feelings. The effect is you do not allow your pendulum of aliveness its full range of motion from one side to the other. Its range remains narrow—your life remains narrow.

Sad to say, there are people who spend all their time in the negative end of emotions, constantly feeling anxious, worried, stressed, nervous—the list is endless. They are still working on the same premise (unconscious though it may be) that they only deserve, and therefore are prepared to let in, only a limited amount of emotion. Some carry a fear that if they allow themselves too much joy and become too high on life their balloon will pop and they will come falling down with a thud. And, it is true, our emotions *are* in constant motion. So, yes, when we are feeling great, it won't last forever. *And* the good part to remember is that when we are at our lowest it too will pass, especially if we recognize that the emotions are a product of our own thoughts, of the particular perspective we are choosing to take. Quiet those and we can be *with* the emotions, rather than let them take us over. We truly can be in charge of our own emotional roller coaster ride.

An important point to stress is that it is normal and part of our human experience to have a broad span of emotions. Having all these emotions doesn't mean we are unstable. We mention this because in many cultures emotions have been given a bad rap. The message from society and the business world is that we are to be rational and logical. Somehow this has been distorted to mean we are not to have or express any emotions. There is a huge difference between making decisions or taking actions based on your reaction to emotions versus feeling and expressing your emotions in a healthy manner. Suppressing our emotions doesn't allow them to be released; letting ourselves feel our emotions fully allows them to pass through us and get processed.

Let's return to the richness—to reiterate, it is being in touch with *all* of yourself...feeling fully, not partially, alive. Each woman will define it and feel it in her own special way. The exercise below will help you connect with the richness that is distinctively yours.

EXERCISE: Uniquely Rich

- *What is richness for you?*
- *What does it look like or feel like to you?*
- *What emotions are you comfortable with?*
- *What emotions do you try to avoid or suppress?*

Spend a little time thinking about how widely your emotional barometer swings. Go back to times when you have been very happy and deeply sad. Sense the intensity of the emotions.

Now think about other occasions when perhaps you restrained yourself more than you would have liked. Recall the times when you did not let yourself completely feel an emotion or allow yourself to express it. Perhaps you were in the company of others and did not have that good full belly laugh you would have liked; perhaps you disguised your anger or sadness.

Let's be clear, this is not about moodiness. You are looking at emotions you choose to feel and those you choose to suppress, along with how you are with them—meaning how you handle them.

Lynn:

First of all you need to know that one of my passions is my dogs. I have had Curly Coated Retrievers for more than twenty years, so they are special to me.

I was on my way to deliver a seminar to a group of educationalists on the same day my best working dog had gone into the vet's for an investigative operation. On my way to the seminar I received the phone call that all dog lovers dread. An inoperable tumor had been found and so I had to make the decision over the phone to let him be put to sleep on the operating table. What a shock to the system.

This was my dilemma: I had not had the opportunity to say goodbye to my dog; there was no way I was going to be able to do so; I had a commitment to deliver a seminar in an hour's time, which called for lots of positive energy. What to do? The one thing I determined to do was not dilute any of the emotions—I was not going to smother up my grief, nor was I going to let my grief get in the way of my enthusiasm for what I was doing. And I was going to be transparent and authentic about it all.

All of this happened within seconds while I was on the phone with the vet. I trusted my vet to let my dog go with respect and that he genuinely would say goodbye on my behalf. I was then able to have a good and full cry in my car, knowing that eventually I would be able to stay with the happy memories of a dog I loved deeply. When I got to my venue I was able to tell the group I was not in a strong place that day and that I was still going to deliver along with my colleague (who was there for me too).

And so it was. I felt as if I was working a whole load of boxes or pigeonholes that I could access whenever I wanted. My focus during the seminar was accessing the energy I required to give the participants what they needed for their learning without feeling that I was in some way betraying my sadness and my loss. At times in the days to come I allowed myself to grieve fully and wholeheartedly without any negative thoughts coming up about being too emotional; I was able to get on with my daily work, talking freely and openly about where I was right then in my life. All this was very new and rich for me. I felt I was dealing with my life in a very purposeful way. On previous occasions I would have lumped everything together, or I'd have put on a good act of hiding my feelings to look good and strong on the surface, and so avoid grieving.

As we've mentioned earlier, richness can be felt not only in the happy times but also in the unhappy times. When you are faced with a tragic situation, embracing your sadness and despair rather than trying to escape from it can give you a sense of richness. This sense of richness can bring you closer to yourself or God (the Universe, Source, Higher Power, Higher Self, Spirit, Mother Earth, however you feel allied to this universal energy) because the experience of surrendering to your sadness and despair is very powerful. Similarly, when you are fully present and genuinely supporting a family member or friend in their time of need or grief, you can feel this same richness resulting from the deeper connection that is being established between you and the other person. Feeling and sharing our deep emotions with others brings us closer to our essence, deepens relationships, and creates this richness we speak of. Think of this the next time things aren't going your way, especially when you or someone close to you is faced with a death, a severe illness, or other tragedy.

Here's an example.

> *Julie:*
>
> Richness is one of the words I use to express an experience of mine that was anything but a happy occasion. The other feelings I had were despair, grief, and helplessness. My oldest son, Steve, and daughter-in-law Shelly were expecting their first baby, our first grandchild. How thrilled we all were, a bundle of joy would be joining the Molner family! However, it wasn't to be.
>
> When my daughter-in-law had the ultrasound to determine the sex of the baby, a fatal kidney condition was uncovered. Instead of celebrating the sex of the baby as we had planned that evening, we sat in shock. Knowing that baby Steven was not going to live filled my heart with much despair. Seeing the agony and grief that my son and his wife had to experience was more than I thought I could bear. Yet I wasn't going to run away from any of the emotions; I jumped in with both feet.
>
> I knew I could not change what was happening and I also knew that I could just "be" and be there for my son and his wife in any way they needed. I was supportive of them while fully feeling my own grief and helplessness…I certainly did not want what was happening to happen but I had no control. There were times I simply allowed myself to lie on the sofa and do nothing but feel my despair, and then there were times when I took action to support them in the way they needed.
>
> When it came time to bury the baby, my son and his wife made certain that all was done with respect and honor. I truly felt and saw the richness that resulted from the authenticity, the sharing of emotions, the togetherness, and the bond that was deepened in the family.
>
> Another time of richness is when I was diagnosed with breast cancer and still in the decision-making process. My first sur-

gery did not rid my breast of all the cancer so I would have to have another surgery—but which type? Lynn came over from the UK for a visit. We spent time doing enjoyable activities and yet there was a cloud over us…it was mine and it was a big one. I experienced so much anxiety, frustration, confusion, anger, and fear—I truly didn't know how I was going to live through it all. I could not see the light at the end of the tunnel because I was at the very entrance. Yet no matter where my emotions took me at any given moment, Lynn was right by my side empathizing and supporting me. I will always remember—it was absolutely *rich* to have her friendship, support, and presence.

Another way to have a rich experience is when you share and express yourself more completely rather than holding back thoughts and ideas for fear of being rejected or judged. We addressed this in Chapter Thirteen—that it is time for you to stand up and be counted, you have the right to speak. So if you have had the tendency to hold back, you now owe it to yourself to practice speaking up, and notice how you feel. Like we've said earlier, if you are not accustomed to speaking your piece, you will probably feel fear or nervousness and that is to be expected. However, afterward, when the emotion of the event and the adrenalin rush have gone, notice the sense of richness, satisfaction, and even freedom that arises. These are the rewards of standing up and saying what you need to say.

We've already taken a look at how we might fear the unknown in an earlier chapter; now you can take a look at the richness of the unknown. Sounds a bit paradoxical, doesn't it? And just as a tragic incident can bring about a feeling of richness, so can fear of the unknown. It all has to do with how we approach it and view it.

First, let's remind ourselves that regardless of whether we are making change or not, we are still living in the unknown. Indeed, what is going to happen in even the next minute is totally unknowable to each and every one of us. So, we can't possibly know what the future holds for us, and this state of not knowing can cause us to feel alive rather than scared. What we need to change is the way we view it, our perspective,—view it in a positive light.

However, more typically, we get hooked into the pattern of life—conforming to what happens "on average" to the "average" person. To coin a phrase, have you ever met anyone with 2.4 kids? We make plans, are accustomed to our lives being a certain way, and we go along our merry way. That is fine except when we become too attached to what we have in our mind. You'll recall the earlier focus on expectations and the exercise you did. Remember, when holding on too tightly to what *we* plan and what *we* are accustomed to, we set ourselves up for disappointments and even sadness or anger—all of this blocks us from feeling the richness of the unknown.

Remaining conscious of the fact that the unknown always exists can change the way you see your life, and therefore change your life. So how are you doing with embracing the truth we expressed in earlier chapters that you've been living with the unknown all your life? Hopefully you are getting the hang of this, and so as you venture into something new that has many unknowns, remember you live in the unknown anyway—it is not so very different. If you choose to step into a state of acceptance, wonder, and curiosity of the unknown, the grip of fear will begin to loosen and you will be open to the richness. After all, think about it, the unknown may hold something beyond your dreams—now that *is* rich!

With a new perspective of the unknown, you can even learn to enjoy it. Not knowing how something is going to turn out; not knowing what a meeting or holiday or event or shopping trip is going to be like from beginning to end can bring out a greater sense of fun, adventure, curiosity. It is all a state of mind, a way of being.

Having childlike curiosity is one way of being that can make a big difference. Children do not run the story ahead of themselves. So instead of trying to figure out what is going to happen or being fearful that you are making a mistake and will fail, let go of the need to control the outcome. Remember, you just might end up with something better than you originally anticipated or were striving for. And, as you were able to see in the previous chapter, you can open the door to more possibilities with this attitude.

 ## EXERCISE: Childlike Curiosity

Try this out for a day and then try it again the next day—taking baby steps until you are more at ease with this new approach, this new way of being:

- *Commit to being curious about everything, dropping assumptions and judgments.*

- *When seeing, hearing, or experiencing everything, first tell yourself that you are stepping into the moment with the eyes and ears of a small child. (Even visualize yourself as a child taking a step into this land of childlike curiosity.)*

- *Think thoughts like, "Hmmm, what will happen if I...?" "What does this feel like?"*

- *Stay open and keep it light instead of serious—have fun and make it a new adventure.*

- *Afterward, notice:*
  - *What impressions and insights came up?*
  - *Was everything as you expected?*
  - *Were there any surprises?*

  Capture these answers in your journal.

Richness is something for us to explore more fully throughout our lives since it can show up in so many varied ways, and each one of us will describe and feel it in our own unique way. Your way of experiencing richness will enliven you and encourage you to continue moving forward with a positive attitude. The more alert you are to the opportunities to experience it, the more you will. Life is a process, and seeking the richness in that process rather than focusing only on the end result affords you endless possibilities—you feel the richness, gain more satisfaction, and enjoy the process of life much more!

CHAPTER TWENTY-TWO

Permission—To Do or Simply Be

*P*ermission, permission, permission...You cannot give yourself too much permission. This is the foundation on which all of the shifts and changes you want to make are built. You must regularly give yourself permission in order to fully access the richness in your life. In fact, giving yourself enough permission is going to be the challenge. As we look more deeply at permission we shall recap some of the key points already made throughout the book.

When did you last give yourself permission to be as outrageous or funny or sensual or lazy as you wanted to be? Let go of the false sense of security you get from clinging to your self-limiting beliefs. All the obstacles and restrictions you place are barriers to your success, to your ability to move onward, your ability to have that truly full and rich life. And these barriers exist only in your thoughts—nowhere else!

Tell yourself it is OK to be you, to choose something new or different and to speak up. Let yourself go—give yourself the permission to feel the richness...to free yourself to live the richness. Actually, it is more than OK; it is your birthright and it's well past due!

It is our choices that show who we are, far more than our abilities.

—J. K. Rowling

197

Permit yourself to follow your urge whatever it may be. Self-expression is innate, particularly as we grow older. The desire to express ourselves, to tell what we have learned, or to give back in some way or another is quite strong in many of us. If you have that urge, remind yourself it is there for a reason or you wouldn't have it. Every time we suppress our urges it is like a mini-death—a death to a little part of us. How can we be fulfilled when we are dying a slow death? Those urges are a part of who you are; do not suppress them!

If you don't truly accept that it is fine for you to have that rich life, to follow your dream, to be the real you, to speak up...you will be forever struggling with self-doubt, disappointment, or guilt. You deserve better!

Ask yourself the following questions right now. Do I fully and truly accept that...

- I can have a rich life?
- I can follow my dream?
- I can be the *real* me?

Pause to hear the answer. If it isn't a resounding *yes* then it's time to get curious about what's still going on for you.

Here's an exercise to help you get stronger in giving yourself permission.

EXERCISE: No Roadblocks

First get a sheet of paper and write down all the reasons why you believe it is wrong to have a rich life, or why you can't give yourself the go-ahead. Then go deeper...now this will require permitting yourself to relax for about twenty minutes. Sit or lie down, turn off the phone, let family or colleagues know you do not want to be disturbed, and block out all other activities. Let yourself get into a meditative, prayer, or relaxed state.

Then ask what is stopping you from giving yourself permission. Don't hang on to the question and do not try to figure it out. Relax and just let the answer surface. If it doesn't, then still let it go. The an-

swer may come up at a later time or day. You can also ask the question again at another time. And here's a good piece of learning. If it doesn't work for you the first time around, please do not consider it a failure. That is old stuff…an old pattern. Some progress will have occurred whether you realize it or not. You may simply need to build up your meditation muscle a bit more!

Continue to write down any reasons you become conscious of. Look at the list and go through them one by one asking yourself if they are true. How many of them are old judgments or self-imposed roadblocks? See if you can dispel them all. Ask for support and verbally process with one of your allies. When you write it and speak it, the power of permission increases.

You do not have to give in to old beliefs and old judgments any longer—you are worthy of the permission and the richness that follows. The boundaries and limitations you may have unwittingly set yourself over the years can go. Allow yourself plenty of wiggle room with loads of permission to follow that dream, go after that desire, be you…get out of that box! Commit to enjoying the journey—your unique journey—and having fun because that is what your day-to-day life is, a journey with marvelous sights for you to see and opportunities awaiting you. You can experience it as you do a scenic road trip or other type of travel. Some of it will be what you anticipated and some may not. Make a pact with yourself to experience the journey with expectancy and curiosity rather than a rigid set of expectations. In other words, keep your eyes, ears, and mind open to what is presented to you because it may be better than what you would have been looking for. Don't block out higher possibilities with a narrow focus; the world is wide open. Do not brush over whatever is in front of you because you don't immediately see the potential. Broaden your mind and your perspective by taking everything that is presented to you into consideration.

Pat (sixty-plus) is a friend and colleague who has continually given herself permission to choose again. Here is a woman who decided on a change of career in her late fifties believing that this would be her last big career step. Pat successfully completed training and certification as a life coach and a great coach she is at that! However she found that it started her on a different track because as it turned out, being a life coach was not for her. This could have been a significant disappointment to her and viewed as a waste of time. Pat however knew that the coaching had come to her for a particular purpose—she just did not yet know what that purpose was.

Various traveling opportunities would arise and loving travel as she does, Pat would give herself permission to take the trips—she got on with the rest of her life and continued to explore. This eventually brought her in touch with an organization that specializes in themed tours. An opportunity arose to become one of their sales consultants, advising possible interested clients, and this is where her coaching skills come to the fore to make her highly successful for this organization.

So, a career as a life coach was not Pat's destination, nor was it her failure—it was merely a station on the journey. And, of course, she still hasn't arrived at her final destination…life is a journey with many stops along the way.

If you get disappointed because everything isn't coming together as you would like or as you expected, or you believe you have failed, that's OK—you can give yourself permission to start over (just like Pat). It's a useful reminder that if as a toddler we had carried these limitations with us about never failing, we'd never have been able to get up and walk! Now how much satisfaction would we have had in life if we had given up as toddlers? Give yourself the freedom and permission to make mistakes—even learn to celebrate the mistakes.

Then try again just like the toddler. Choose a positive perspective; take a close look and you will walk away with new learning from your perceived mistake.

> *Be bold. If you're going to make an error, make a doozey, and don't be afraid to hit the ball.*
>
> —Billie Jean King

If you have difficulty giving yourself permission to make a mistake or to just be yourself, here's a story that shows how you can start with the smaller events.

Julie:

Most of my life I have been challenged with being a perfectionist. Oh yes, I had to get things done and get them done the "right" way! I analyzed everything so that I could make improvements, be more efficient, take care of my family and home better. I followed endless lists…get the picture? It was a compulsion, a coping skill I developed early on in life. You can imagine the reputation I had—"Julie doesn't make mistakes, she has everything under control."

As I was approaching the age of fifty I realized that trying to do everything right was wearing me down—I was tired, *very* tired of working so hard and I wanted more fun. In fact I always did have this little voice inside that said, "I just want to have fun," yet I had to get things done first. I admired people who seemed to be freer and more spontaneous than I was. Finally I chose to take action to change—it wasn't going to happen all by itself. I had to teach myself permission to let go and I started by making a conscious effort to loosen up with some of the smaller things. I accepted that it was OK to make mistakes—I knew that perfection doesn't exist, so why waste precious time striving for it?

The day that stands out in my mind was a Saturday afternoon late in May. I had the usual errands to run and an extra one, which was to pick up an ice cream cake for my husband's birthday. When I returned home from all the errands, I emptied my car of everything and then started some household chores. Well, about three hours later I opened the freezer to get something and noticed the ice cream cake was not there. "Oh my gosh," I thought, "where is the cake?" I stood there for a moment totally perplexed and then ran out to my car. There it was, still in the box on the floor of the backseat—all turned to mush. It was a hot, sunny afternoon—a very beautiful day!

Instead of being upset, I gave myself full permission to goof up! I was delighted and broke into a huge belly laugh, and continued laughing as I drove back to the store to buy another cake. It felt good—it was OK to make the mistake. This was a turning point for me—I was relieved that I could finally let go to the point of wasting a good cake, money, time…all the things I would normally fret over. And besides being OK with the mistake, I celebrated by telling everyone about it over the next few days and even months later. I was proud that I broke through my self-imposed barrier; it was all about giving myself the permission that I deserved, permission to be me—mistakes and all!

Just like the baby who takes one step at a time, we too achieve personal growth by doing the same—taking one step at a time or one mistake at a time. Notice where you may be able to give yourself more permission…again, you can start with small things.

As you "show up" more and more and enrich your life, you will be inspiring your family, friends, and others to permit themselves to follow their own path and acquire their own richness. What a gift you'll be giving to others. How many times have you seen someone who has allowed herself to be a certain way or do something and you've walked away wishing you could too. How about the times where the light went on and you said to yourself, "Hey, I can too," and you moved on it. That's what we are talking about. The more others see you give yourself permission, then they can begin to see it is fine for them also. Now, isn't that rich?

Sometimes feelings of jealousy arise—either in yourself or in another person. Here's a tip. Check out the thoughts that are causing this emotion. There's something there to be uncovered. Is this person behaving in a way that you don't allow for yourself because you judge it as bad, inappropriate, or not permissible? Is there an aspect of you that you are denying and judging? Take a closer look at where you give yourself the permission and where you don't. If you notice another person being jealous of you, remember, this stems from *their* self-limiting thoughts.

As we have already said, making choices has consequences. Giving yourself permission to design the life you want is making a choice and with such permission comes responsibility for the consequences. Some of the consequences will be all bright and wonderful—and then there will be some consequences you simply couldn't or didn't count on happening.

Such consequences are inevitable and if you anticipate them do not allow them to prevent you from making the choice in the first place. Doing this only leads to stasis. Instead, be ready to accept what happens; step forward and clean up any messes that may result.

When you redesign your own life it will impact other people…and they may not like what they see. We've said this before. You need to remember their dissatisfaction or unhappiness is their stuff. Messes are created as a result of the differences in viewpoint, perspective, and reality that arise between you and the other person involved. By sticking around to clear up the mess through listening and talking compassionately with the other person, your life experience will be all the richer. Yet under no circumstances are you to take on their unhappiness as your own.

It is crucial that you are OK with your choices so that the mess remains separate from your choice. If you can do this it prevents what happens to so many people: They decide on a change (major or minor, it doesn't matter), start to make the change, a mess is created, and instead of hanging around to clean up the "poop," they get scared, walk away from it, and stop the change. Do not give up because of a mess—messes are bound to happen when making changes. Give yourself the permission to let them occur, deal with them, learn from them, and then keep moving forward.

Staying true to yourself when choosing, following your urges and dreams, speaking up, not quitting when the going seems tough, cleaning up the mess—these and so much more will contribute to your sense of self-worth, your self-satisfaction, and the fullness of your life. See for yourself—it's all rich.

I don't need anyone to rectify my existence. The most profound relationship we will ever have is the one with ourselves.

—Shirley MacLaine

CHAPTER TWENTY-THREE

Freedom—One of the Greatest Riches We Can Have in Our Life

W ith permission comes freedom—it is truly a rich experience to have freedom. What are we referring to specifically when we say freedom? We think everyone of our generation can relate to what freedom must have meant for someone like Nelson Mandela after so many years of imprisonment. As you might imagine, we are not looking at that kind of freedom here. We are talking about releasing yourself from the "prison" of your own mindset, the old belief system we've talked about before from which only you can release yourself. You have the key and every right to liberate yourself to more richness and freedom.

Yes, freedom to create the life you want and be truly "at choice." Freedom to totally release any inner turmoil that exists and let go of the struggling you've done with the "shoulds" versus your desires. The struggle has kept the richness and your authenticity at bay...maybe at times it's been within your reach but never quite fully yours. You are now ready to claim it.

Having completed the exercises, you will have more clarity on who you are at your core, what is possible for you, and what is holding you back. All this introspection is an ongoing process and a practice to follow the rest of your life. You live in a dynamic, constantly changing scene. As you grow into who you really are, you will find there is still more self-awareness and clarity to seek. Your current thoughts and feelings are complex; it has taken a lifetime to develop them. The more you are aware, understand, and love yourself, the more you can question and choose to dispel any of the beliefs or illusions that no longer serve you in the new reality you want to create. As you gain more self-awareness, you will have more freedom of choice; you'll be better equipped to make the choices that work for you, not against you.

As we see it, freedom means consciously realizing at all times that you have a choice. Being free from old habits and unconscious reactions so you can make purposeful choices on a day-to-day basis—this is true freedom. Allow yourself the freedom to discover who you are, to do what makes your heart sing, and to make choices that are best for you. Recognize that you do have a choice as opposed to being in denial and claiming that you are at the mercy of another, society, the "shoulds," etc. As we've pointed out in earlier chapters, your friends and family may not all agree or be on board immediately with your new choices—and in time they will adjust. If not, they may not be meant to be with you. Whatever it is they are objecting to is about their perspective—what they are choosing to think, not about you personally. This is something you must remember.

Imagine you've just declared a new change to someone you know and she/he explodes saying, "You can't do that, it's totally selfish!" Spend a few minutes reflecting on what the thinking behind her/his outburst might be. Remember, the root of it is always about the person doing the thinking and exploding. When you can sense the quality of someone's thinking, you can then see them more compassionately and not get hooked by reacting defensively.

With freedom comes the responsibility of authenticity…being the real "you" and doing what comes from within, that yearning to be or to do from which you can no longer turn away.

Earlier in the book when you experienced your essence, it animated your subconscious about who you are at your core.

Getting acquainted with your essence, the "being" rather than the "doing," can open your eyes to a part of you that you haven't connected with. It allows your subconscious to show you your inner desire to move onto another plane. Touching base with the real "you" is an effective way to help you clarify those dreams and desires. So, after you have found your true essence and can access her in any given moment, make it part of your routine to visit her and reconnect. There is usually a great sense of knowingness, of wisdom about this person. Remember, she is already within you…you can start to be her now. You can free yourself to imagine what "she" would choose, how "she" would dress, and how "she" would respond. Check in with her—you'll see that integrating with her can have you feeling more satisfaction, more of that richness.

What if the question is not why am I so infrequently the person I want to be, but why do I so infrequently want to be the person I really am.

—Oriah Mountain Dreamer

Julie:
 In my early fifties I knew I did not want to continue with my career as an account manager in the automotive industry. Although I truly liked my co-workers, my customers, and certain aspects of my job, I knew in my heart it was not the place for me, but I had *no* idea what else I would do. I kept my eyes open and eventually found a workshop that Rick Jarow was conducting at the Esalen Institute in California titled "Creating the Work You Love." The title of this workshop (which is the same as his book) called to me—so I went.

As it turned out, the workshop was totally different from what I expected. We focused on inner work and personal growth, which was indeed something I needed and enjoyed doing but I didn't quite understand how this would help me find my new career. The final piece of the workshop was a meditation in which we were to receive an answer to a question that went something like, "What can I do that I can live with for the next six months?" When the meditation was over, I was extremely disappointed because all I got was a visual of two words in bright neon lights—"BE AUTHENTIC." I whined about not having what I considered to be a clear-cut answer. For weeks, my reaction was "Where the heck is this going to get me?"

Well, after a couple of months of practicing authenticity, I finally "got" it and when I did it became crystal clear to me. If I was authentic, then the "real" me—who I was at my core—and what I was meant to do would appear. How simple and yet how challenging. Through the subsequent months and years I followed the thought of becoming more and more authentic, and in three years I became a life coach and left my previous job. Being authentic has opened my professional and personal life to many great joys I would not otherwise have experienced and it led me to writing this book with Lynn!

Authenticity is honoring your values, standing tall and speaking up for what you believe and what you desire. We are referring to the true essence of who you are as a person, what you believe and care about. Authenticity is indeed that full self-expression with responsibility we talked about earlier.

Think about this statement: Being authentic is the answer to what most of us are seeking. How else will you ever feel the most fulfilled and satisfied? Your authenticity is where your yearnings, desires, talents, and joy reside. Reflect on this further—it is logical.

What might transpire for you if you were more authentic? What awaits the real you?

We do not mean that being authentic is saying or doing *anything* that is on your mind. As an example, someone who is angry and shouting at others is not being authentic. That type of behavior is due to a lack of self-management, of not being in a good place, of having poor quality thinking and not being responsible for the impact created.

As you will already have guessed, authenticity has its rewards and it also has risks. Some people will like you and others will not. You need to please yourself first and foremost because it is certain you can't please everyone, no matter what. And if you find yourself trying to do that, it's a good reminder that you have taken yourself out of the driver's seat of your own life. Being authentic and in the driver's seat of your life is crucial in bringing forth richness. If you are living your life in the passenger seat, you are not truly living your own life—how can it be rich? How can you feel fulfillment? Although taking the first steps in being authentic can feel like you are standing naked in the middle of the street and shouting out to everyone, "Look at me, I'm naked!" it is worth it. Ask yourself if being authentic is a scary prospect for you.

> *Even the fear of death is nothing compared to the fear of not having lived authentically and fully.*
>
> —Frances Moore Lappé

Think of women you admire who stick their neck out and say and do what they believe in. They exhibit freedom *and* they take a risk each time. We will use Oprah as an example. She is said to be one of the most powerful women in the world, and continues to grow and learn about herself while sharing it with the public. Many people adore her. Whatever your view, Oprah embraces freedom. She has learned to accept herself and be herself even in front of millions of people. She has strong opinions, which she is willing to express without fearing loss of popularity. Can you imagine what that might feel like? Yes, maybe scary but oh, what freedom…indeed it is Oprah's freedom to be authentic that has brought her popularity and fame and allowed her to make a difference in the lives of so many people.

> *Before you agree to do anything that might add even the smallest amount of stress to your life, ask yourself: What is my truest intention? Give yourself time to let a yes resound within you. When it's right, I guarantee that your entire body will feel it.*
>
> —Oprah Winfrey

EXERCISE: Body Awareness

This exercise brings you back to body awareness—of letting the knowing that is in every cell of your body express itself. Physical awareness helps realization and learning.

Take out your journal and write the insights you gain from the following questions. Don't discount anything; pay attention to the urges, the sensations that come up for you. Let your intuition and your body give you the messages. Do not let rational and analytical thought get in your way.

- *What is your experience of the freedom to be you? It can be different for each woman.*

- *Sit in a position that represents this freedom; notice for a few moments what that is like.*

- *Now stand in a position that embodies the freedom to be you. What is that like?*

- *What is possible for you from these positions?*

- *Do some daydreaming; what pops up?*

Draw upon your insights to free yourself, and regularly practice sitting and standing in the positions that provide you a feeling of freedom in order to empower yourself.

Authenticity also brings many rewards. There are so many more advantages for you and for others. Perhaps the greatest advantage of all is that your inner turmoil ceases and is replaced with greater self-acceptance and peace. You will be more at ease and comfortable in varied situations knowing who you are rather than trying to "be someone" or be the way you think you're "supposed" to be.

Lynn:

In my previous career I used to think I had to make an impression—dress correctly, make an impact by speaking, impress people with what I knew. Well, this is what you expect from teachers, isn't it? And so I carried it over even more into my life as a senior manager, taking this belief about appearances with me. The real "me" could never be seen—I was not from the "right" background, did not have the "right" qualifications, did not speak with the "right" accent, and so on....So when things didn't go according to plan—my plan—I felt awful, a failure.

Because I was convinced the problem lay with me, the result was that the next time I had to try even harder...and when it didn't work, the sense of failure was even stronger and the "fall" even harder. This was a downward spiral that made life seem like hard work. But I'm a hard worker, ambitious, and not easily deterred. And it took its toll.

Through the work that I have done on myself I have learned to be me. I know the impact I have, I know the gift I bring to any setting, I know when I need to speak, and most importantly of all I know it's OK if I don't. If I choose to become part of the wallpaper, that's OK too. I'm free, yes, free to be me...and no need to compete with anyone else!

When you are authentic and free, not only will you feel peace and acceptance, so will others in your presence. Whatever you do or however you choose to be has an impact on others, whether you are acquainted with them or not, whether you intend the impact or not. You can have an impact on someone even if you never see them or know of them. How wonderful to know that your impact is one of authenticity. Others will also begin to feel the freedom to be "real": "If she can do it, I guess I can too."

> *Let the world know you as you are, not as you think you should be, because sooner or later, if you are posing, you will forget the pose, and then where are you?*
>
> —Fanny Brice

One of the most wonderful things is that we all, each and every one of us, know deep down who or how we want to be as we move through life's journey. You will get a glimpse of who this is when you allow yourself to bring your dreams alive.

Another aspect of freedom, you will recall, is that you have the freedom to decide who you want to have in your circle of friends, without anger or malice. You can be free to keep friends or release them—allow yourself to choose the people who lift you up rather than bring you down. It's also the time to notice who is missing from your life. Who would make your life even richer if they were a part of it?

Doesn't it just make sense that when you are choosing with freedom, life will become richer?

This newfound freedom will bring high levels of consciousness and greater aliveness to you. It is self-perpetuating…you will be able to make more and more good choices. You can be free from the old worn-out rules—free to spread your wings and fly from the "nest" (or prison) you've held yourself in.

CHAPTER TWENTY-FOUR

Savor Life—
It Tastes Real Good!

Savor life! What does that mean to you? To us it means to thoroughly relish, enjoy, and delight in all aspects of our day-to-day existence. Have you ever given much thought to what you savor and how much time you take to savor? With a quiet mind and a high level of consciousness, you can savor many things that normally go unnoticed. Choosing to savor as much as possible and as often as possible leads to that life we speak of, the one that is richer than you've ever imagined. So much more is available to you when you open your mind and savor.

By "savoring" we mean being consciously present with what you are doing right now in every moment of every day regardless of what it is, whether you consider it to be enjoyable or decidedly not enjoyable. You may well be saying to yourself, "Well, of course I am conscious of what I am doing." Yes, you certainly are awake when taking action; however, it is quite likely that some aspects of these actions—very often those you do literally without thinking, go entirely unnoticed. A good example for many of us is when we are preparing to leave our home. We instinctively put overcoats on if it is cold; we instinctively turn off the lights, unlock and lock the front door. How many times have you functioned in automatic mode and later wondered if you had done any of these things? What a relief to know this forgetfulness cannot be put down to senility, but rather to the skill you have developed over many years, of smoothing over what is actually happening and letting your brain go on autopilot. It's a great device but it does mean you miss a good proportion of your life.

The act of savoring brings you right into the *now*, and *now* is where you make choices that influence the future that you truly want. Be present in the moment and notice what you find.

Practice being in the present and learn to take in the small pleasures: the sun shining in your window, the color of the sky as the sun is setting, the shapes of the clouds, the sound of the rain, the feel of wind upon your face, the sound of the birds singing, the antics of squirrels...take time to savor all these things and *more*. Stop to listen to the sound of children laughing and giggling, and adults too. Savor the smile on a loved one's face or on the face of a stranger.

Enjoy the small pleasures of your life, like taking a shower. Feel the warmth of the water hitting your body, notice how different parts of your body feel—this can be utterly delightful! Choose the temperature of water that is just right for you and pamper yourself.

Give yourself a body and/or a scalp massage if you are washing your hair. Take a few moments to massage your skin and scalp while paying attention to the sensations; grant yourself a treat to start the day. What is that like compared to jumping in the shower, scrubbing away while your thoughts are racing in all directions, and then hopping out again? It only takes a couple more minutes to free your thoughts as you concentrate on savoring the showering experience.

Perhaps you enjoy soaking in a hot bath...maybe later in the day or in the evening...go for it. Carve out time for solitude, light some candles, turn out the lights, and slip into the tub making sure to have an inflatable pillow or towel to cushion your neck and head. Lie back, close your eyes, and feel your body warmed by the water; feel the shifting water against your skin as you move your arms and hands. Feel your body loosen and relax...savor and enjoy!

At bedtime what about slowly getting into bed with clean sheets, intentionally feeling the smoothness and coolness of the sheets against your skin? How about the softness or firmness of your mattress, the comfort of it? Hmmm, imagine indulging yourself. It's a much nicer way to get ready for a good night's sleep, as opposed to flopping yourself into the bed and not feeling anything, just waiting for sleep to come because you are feeling exhausted or have a busy day tomorrow.

And what about one of our favorite events in life—eating! Yes, sitting down and slowly eating a meal or a snack. So often we do not fully taste and experience even our most favorite foods and treats because of the speed with which we eat. Slow down and taste your favorite food in a way you perhaps haven't before.

It's great to do this with something you love to eat—maybe a chocolate or some other candy, a piece of fruit, a cup of coffee, or a steak. It doesn't matter what it is.

EXERCISE: Same Thing, New Taste

The next time you are going to eat a particular food, prepare yourself. Look at it carefully from all angles; see its beauty even before you start to taste it. Smell its aroma whether it's light or pungent. How near to it do you need to get? How does its aroma change as you get closer? How does it feel as you hold it in your hands? Now prepare yourself for your first mouthful. Notice if and how much you are salivating, how much you are able to anticipate the wonderful taste you are about to enjoy.

What do you feel on your tongue and the roof of your mouth? What is the texture like? If it's something you are going to bite through, feel the sensation as your teeth penetrate the food and release the taste. Let the taste burst through into your mouth.

Now enjoy the chewing—notice the crunchiness or smoothness of the chew. Notice the way it helps exude more flavor. Does the taste change from that first delightful burst to something more mature as you chew?

And as you prepare to swallow, sense the food's movement downward into your digestive system, knowing it will be carrying on its work of sustaining you.

Go with the flow and see what else you can detect about the food. Can you taste all the different flavors that go to make up your favorite food? It's all about taking the time to take in the food and chew it thoroughly, tasting rather than gulping it down while so deeply in conversation that you do not even notice what you are eating (or how much, for that matter).

As we've said, it is common for us to have our thoughts elsewhere or rush through an experience rather than be in the *now*. Here are a few other ways in which we can miss out on savoring.

How many times have you felt you have missed a performance by one of your kids because you were nervous about how they would fare? Anticipating what might go wrong, you lost the experience. Have you ever visited places, stopped to take photos of the famous spot, and then turned around and left? What didn't you see because you were focused on moving on to the next place?

The "next place" is where so much of our thoughts and focus are placed. It's one thing to have plans; it is another to be focused so much on where we are headed that we lose where we are right now. The same is true of the past. It is fine to think about what we can learn from the past, how we can improve. However, we are wasting time and missing the present when we ruminate or stew about something that happened in the past. It is no longer a reality—it exists only in our thoughts.

One effective method that helps bring us into the *now* so we can savor even the ordinary is mindfulness. When we say mindful we mean to focus intently on what is at hand in the moment right now, as opposed to being in the autopilot mode. It is a way to prevent missing out on what we are engaged in. When we are in this mode, we can shift our mood and perception. To be mindful is to stop thinking of other things, such as what happened earlier in the day or how we are going to get everything accomplished. Consciously choose mindfulness to pull you into the present moment, the here and now so you can experience every moment of your life. You can learn how to be mindful and in the *now* by saying exactly what you are doing either out loud or silently in your mind. This practice is great for calming and focusing the mind. The example below clarifies how this is done and how effective it can be. Try it next time you are doing a routine task.

Julie:

I will always remember a day quite a few years ago when practicing mindfulness made a dramatic difference to my state of mind, and how my entire day changed thereafter. I was rushing (which was quite the norm for me) and felt overwhelmed with all the things I expected myself to do. I had just gotten home from the grocery store and since I had been putting in many hours at work, in my mind I wasn't getting things done in my personal life. I was anything but in the mood to be unloading groceries. I was tired and viewed my task as a bother.

Suddenly I realized this attitude was getting me nowhere so I decided to practice mindfulness. Since no one else was home, I spoke out loud (of course, now even if someone else is home, I'll speak out loud if I want to). This is a sampling of what I was saying: "I am picking up this can of soup from the bag and now I am placing it on the shelf. I am now taking a box of crackers from the bag and placing it on the shelf." Within two or three minutes, and I am not exaggerating, a shift occurred. My thoughts changed 180 degrees….I began thinking of how fortunate I was to have the food to unload and how grateful I was for it and everything else I had. From this simple exercise, I went from being frustrated and stuck in "what's next" to savoring the moment…savoring my life. A lighthearted feeling came over me and I approached the remainder of the day and evening with joy instead of self-imposed misery.

Please allow yourself a full experience of savoring. Here's an exercise to help you deepen the practice you've already started.

EXERCISE: Even More Savoring!

Commit to setting aside at least half an hour—an hour would be even better. Choose a time when you will be least likely to be confronted with something important that will stop you from doing this, a time you will not be interrupted. You can take moments here and there to savor, and we are emphatic about that—anytime you are able do so, you will benefit. Yet when you spend an extended period of time is when you will feel a dramatic difference and sense a greater richness, the richness we are talking about. It takes time for our minds to relax and settle in, so give yourself the time.

Choose a favorite spot in nature—a park, beach, trail, wherever it may be. Go there alone.

- *Do not speak with anyone, remain silent; be with yourself and with nature.*

- *Walk slowly and observe all that is along your path stopping to look closely at anything that catches your eye—not judging it, just noticing—the small and the big.*

- *Find a spot to sit…on the ground, on a tree trunk, a bench; simply look at everything with the intention of seeing the details you've never noticed before.*

- *Notice the pattern of the clouds in the sky and the shade of blue in the sky, and how it contrasts to what is around you.*

- *Look at the different components that make up your view—blades of grass, leaves, grains of sand, stones, pebbles, etc. Be curious. What do you notice about them that you haven't before?*

- *What patterns and shapes do you see?*

- *Are there any insects flying or crawling about? Observe them and their activity.*

- *Relax and enjoy being a part of nature. How connected are you to nature? What value do you get from nature?*

If you find your thoughts wandering (as indeed you will), be gentle with yourself and bring your focus back to where you are right now, what you are observing, even start saying to yourself what you are doing. It brings a whole new meaning to "talking to trees."

Afterward, review your experience by writing in your journal the new insights you gained. You can begin to integrate your insights into your regular routine, your everyday lifestyle. Your consciousness and therefore your awareness have expanded and we hope you now realize how much more you can bring into your life, how much more richness there is for you.

After you've carried out these exercises, notice the time. As we savor, time can seem to stand still—a real step toward that richer life.

Being open and free of judgment can bring us richness in the most unexpected ways. Take something like sitting at an outdoor café or waiting for your flight in an airport. Watch the world go by without any judgment about the people who are passing, the clothes they are wearing, the way they walk, and how they behave. Simply observing and being curious about these people—who they are, what they might be doing, and how they are enjoying themselves—can make for a very interesting learning experience. Raise your consciousness about what you are seeing, the colors, the smells, the noises—all free from any judgment. Do you see that being in the *now* without judgment enlivens your experiences a notch or two? How much more is available to you from this place?

We are also suggesting that you might try even *more* savoring with those tasks you don't like and want to get over as quickly as possible. Savoring is not just about liking what you are doing. It is about not missing out on anything that goes on in your life on a day-by-day, hour-by-hour basis. We repeat, it is your life we are talking about—all those day-by-day, hour-by-hour activities are your life whether or not you enjoy what you are doing. Don't miss out on your life by being on autopilot!

EXERCISE: Savor the Unsavory

This is an exercise to savor the 'unsavory'! Yes, look at savoring something you do not normally like doing.

Think of a chore or activity that definitely is not your favorite. It may be something you do regularly; it may be one of your "must do's" such as visiting distant relatives; it may be getting stuck in a traffic jam. You can choose—we just know you will have something you don't particularly enjoy!

The next time you are preparing to do this activity or chore, choose to savor it. This does not just mean consciously doing it much more slowly—though this helps. It means having all your senses alerted to feeling and experiencing the activity.

The question you need to keep asking yourself over and over again as you do your chosen task is "What's new for me?" "What can I taste, see, smell, hear, touch, experience that I haven't noticed before?" It can be a real sensual experience in the true meaning of the word.

If you find your mind wandering and it just becomes a slow, mechanical exercise while you are off elsewhere in your head, bring yourself gently back to where you are by saying to yourself exactly what it is you are doing. As we've said before, this is a great way to turn off the mind chatter.

Do not hurry. You may be pleasantly surprised to see that time has passed in a full and interesting way and you've completed the task just as quickly.

A friend of ours, Pauline, spent a great deal of time in the "duty" place of seeing her parents. She never had a good relationship with her mother. Pauline was carrying the burden many of us do of feeling that she was never good enough and therefore was a disappointment to her parents.

Consequently, making the journey to see her parents was a chore; she just wanted to get it over with and get back home.

As Pauline went through her own personal growth process she was able to step more and more into who she is. This meant allowing herself to fulfill her own dreams without thoughts of what her mother might think—especially if her ideas failed. She now knows how to be with failure for she sees it clearly as just another learning process.

The more she has given herself space to grow, the more her relationship with her mother has grown and developed into something that is now quite special. There is a depth of understanding that had not been there for more than thirty years. Of course, her mother has not changed dramatically—it's our friend who has. Pauline has been able to shift to a stronger position for herself and see her mother with nonjudgmental love and compassion. She now savors the time she spends with her aging mother rather than dreading it. In so doing she has let more fulfillment enter her life—and her mother's.

So it's possible to savor the whole of your life—in every moment, at every twist and turn. It's made much easier if you have a quiet mind, free of intruding personal thoughts that create a negative energy for you. If your mind is quiet, your consciousness is raised, permitting you to see much more clearly what is going on—and keep it free from judgment.

Is it obvious enough how enthusiastic we are about getting you to savor? Because of our enthusiasm you may think we are experts and savor from morning till night on a daily basis. Well, no, we don't. Just like you, we have to remind ourselves to stop and savor, remember to slow down and pay attention to the now and delight in the present. The more each of us practices it, the more naturally it will come, and yet realistically life does get in the way many times.

Maintaining a strong intention and not letting go of that intention will allow you to seize the opportunities to savor whatever it is you are doing. Bringing your awareness to it and choosing to savor is all that is needed—the result will be that richer life we are talking about.

CHAPTER TWENTY-FIVE

Celebrate—There Are More Reasons Than You Think!

A joyful way to bring about a life richer than you've ever imagined is to *celebrate*. It is customary to celebrate only the larger events, like birthdays, graduations, weddings, newborn babies, and religious holidays. However, there is so much more to celebrate in life. Celebration is about gratitude—gratitude for the "beingness" of life. So it's important to make your celebration aligned with what feels energetically right for you. Celebrate all your successes, no matter how small. Celebrate every change and effort you make. Even celebrate what you consider to be a failure. Most of all, celebrate *you* for you are a woman of substance who does not take things for granted!

> *The lovely thing about being me is that I am so damn good at it!*
>
> —Michele Agnew

Everything about you can be celebrated. Do you ever feel appreciative on any given day because things have gone so well for you? You will now realize that you are in charge of how well you perceive things to have gone, and most importantly, how much appreciation you feel.

In order to have that truly rich life it is essential for you to celebrate all you experience because that *is* your life.

> *The more you praise and celebrate your life, the more there is in life to celebrate.*
>
> —Oprah Winfrey

You probably celebrate other events from time to time—usually the considerable successes such as landing that new job, getting a raise or bonus, or making that long-awaited sale. Most of us let other events slip right by because we view them as insignificant or not very noteworthy. We *expect* ourselves to accomplish or succeed to a certain degree on a regular basis; by doing so we diminish ourselves.

Think of very young children when they draw a picture or make something and then run to their parents with glee saying, "Look what I made!" They, along with their parents, are delighted and joyful at the child's new action. If you are a mother, remember how you fussed over all the activities of your children, how you encouraged or cheered them on no matter how small or simple their accomplishment. I'm sure many of you who are mothers have celebrated when your child first learned to use the potty. What a celebration that has been in many households! Well, one could say, "What's the big deal?" Yet it *is* a big deal, for it is new and a first and many times scary for that child. Celebrating a child's achievement is a way of honoring the child and honoring life. Why do we lose this simple joy, this appreciation of success? We fully believe that you as an adult deserve the same and you can begin by celebrating *you*.

Therefore, taking any step that is new for you and that requires courage is a reason to celebrate *you*. For example, it may be that you want to call a school or college about a class but you continue to put it off. You have some trepidation...not sure if you want to take the class, don't know if you can handle it...all the resistant thoughts that swirl around your mind. If you make the phone call to obtain information, it is a step forward and worth celebrating. Recognize that although the step may look small, since it is *new*, it is big. If there is some fear around it, then it's even bigger. Make sense? Whenever you make a change and do some growth work, it is worthy of acknowledgment and celebration. You are making an effort just like that child and you have good reason to honor yourself for it.

Whether or not the step you've taken appears to be a big deal to someone else is not relevant. No one else is in your shoes; you know what the big efforts are in your life. As we have said before, it is crucially important not to get hooked into comparing yourself with others, with what others seem to do so readily. You cannot be in their reality. Everyone has their own challenges. The big question is, "Do you have the guts to face yours, do something about them, and then celebrate?" It's your choice!

> ### Julie:
>
> Three years ago I followed a strong urge to become a shaman, which is obviously not mainstream. It also meant going away from home for a week or so at a time in order to study. I very much wanted my family as allies in this process—yet my impression was that my sons thought Mother was being a little whacky again doing something that was a bit of a laugh. I believed this was largely due to the jokes my husband would make about what I was doing. Although he supported me and meant no harm, his joking left me feeling diminished and undermined. I believed that my daughter was the only one in the family who supported me 100 percent in this venture.
>
> I finally decided my first step toward changing this situation was to request that my husband take me seriously and not joke about anything I was doing, at all. Of course I realized it was my "stuff" and I wanted him to know his impact when I was feeling less than secure. This took courage because I do enjoy his humor and did not want to hurt his feelings. I then drummed up the courage to have a private conversation with

each of my sons, Steve and Eric, to request that they also take me seriously regarding my commitment to undergo shaman training. I needed them to understand how important the training was to me and how important it was for me to feel that I had their support, rather than their ridicule.

They had no idea that I carried this impression; they were in fact surprised by it and were extremely supportive of what I was doing, as well as having the conversation with them. I also told them about my intent to coauthor this book with Lynn. It was heartwarming to learn my sons and their wives, Shelly and Tara, believed in me and my abilities to coauthor a book. So by naming what I felt uncomfortable with I was able virtually immediately to dissipate any fears I was holding. I cleared my mind and learned that the fears were based on *my* perception—the story I had made up in *my* mind. I am still grateful to them for having the conversations with me and for everyone's support.

For someone else these family conversations may seem simple; however, for me it was *huge*. I do have what I consider to be a close and loving relationship with my sons. However, I am neither in the habit of requesting what I need from them nor asking them to take time from their busy lives just for me. Filled with relief, I celebrated by sharing the incident with several friends and allies—for me sharing is fulfilling. And since I love music and dancing, I carved out time to listen and dance to some favorite music in my living room—all by myself—yes, that too is something that delights me!

Celebrating can take many forms…as we stated, the usual ones we think of are throwing a big party, dining at a special restaurant, taking a special trip, etc. All of those and others are well and good and do go ahead with them (we certainly would not talk you out of that). We are also asking you to celebrate in other ways, ways that may be simple (or not), yet significant to you. Perhaps some of your savoring activities can also be celebrations. As examples: giving yourself a special treat to a day spa, or lying in the bath surrounded by candles and listening to soothing music, taking time out during a busy schedule for a treat like eating and thoroughly savoring a double chocolate muffin.

How about celebrating yourself by wearing a color or a style of clothing that is not the norm for you; clothing you just love but have always said, "Oh, that's too bold for me" or "It isn't me." Well, dare to do it! Plan an afternoon for some amusement; ask a friend to go with you to buy an outfit, a friend you see as somewhat bold. Intentionally set up the shopping trip as a special event…what way would turn this previous scary step into one that is amusing and fun for you? And when you wear the clothes…what will make that special for you too?

There are even more approaches to celebrating, very simple ones that do not take time and effort. Your individuality and creativity can help you come up with various ideas that will be special for you and maybe even fun. To get your thoughts going, here are a few suggestions: stop for a moment or two to think of your accomplishment; put a smile on your face and tell yourself "good job" or "I'm proud of myself." Get into a victory posture and say "Yeah!" Let yourself have fun with this—do a little dance, sing a little song—do what makes your heart sing.

Any action you take, any behavior you change, whether it is doing something or stopping yourself from an old habit, it is new to *you*. It does not matter that it is something everyone else appears to be able to do (or so you may tell yourself). Just like the child who drew a new picture or the toddler learning to walk, it was a huge achievement.

These are not frivolous requests we are making of you; we are serious. Have a special manicure, pedicure, or massage (especially if you're not accustomed to having one); enjoy a real treat that is out of the ordinary for you. Buy something you wouldn't normally buy—something that has meaning for you, that represents the success or is in celebration of who you are and who you are becoming. You could buy a scarf, earrings, pin, trinket, flowers, whatever speaks to you. If it is not the norm at your home, how about turning down the lights and having a candlelit dinner with your family, spouse, significant other *or* by yourself? When you next have a glass of wine, try to refrain from simply saying "Cheers!" Think of something you have accomplished and salute that. All of these are suggestions—*you* know what would be a celebration for you!

Stop right here. Throughout the book you have been building toward change and shift—something different you want to see in your life. You have identified your allies who, in their different ways, will support you in getting there. You will have openly articulated your intention. How did you celebrate this huge step and the many others you have taken? If you did not celebrate, write down twenty ways you are going to celebrate how far you've come since you started this book, and plan to put each one into action.

Even when you consider something a failure, celebrate. The action you took served a good purpose. It proved that it was not the best path for you; it wasn't going to bring you the richness you deserve, or it may simply be indicating that it is not yet the right time. Don't hide your failure; own it and understand that it didn't work for you. You weren't "wrong"—it was merely something to be eliminated. As Thomas Edison stated, "If I find 10,000 ways something won't work, I haven't failed. I am not discouraged because every wrong attempt discarded is often a step forward...."

Your failure may be a stepping stone to something better, a signal to reevaluate your plans, or permission to say, "No, not that but (something else)." You may have an "aha" and see that you are to turn and go in a totally different direction; ultimately the "failure" may lead you in a more meaningful direction—one that could very well turn out to be the best direction. Reward yourself for having the courage to take these steps to move forward no matter how things turn out; it is your courage you are celebrating. Honor it! (A little reminder here…if there is no fear, there is no courage.)

How about this?

Dare to imagine! Dare to do! Dare to achieve!

What did that old Nike commercial say? "Just do it!"

An incentive game you can play is to prepare your own "celebration" cards in advance. "What?" you may say. And we say, "Yes!" What is it you imagine and envision? Jump ahead a couple of months and visualize that you have done it and you have achieved it. No matter how small a step it is, know that it is significant; nothing is too small especially when starting out! Now take some file cards or whatever you prefer. Draw, color, have fun with your creativity on these cards and write down congratulations to yourself. Or simply buy yourself some cards—the type you would absolutely love to receive and send them to yourself!

Sue, another of our clients, has discovered great joy in writing and through many iterations (such is the change process) she has decided what she wants to do is to write a book. It feels like a mammoth task—and a long-term one at that.

During a visualization session she was able to get to a day of celebration two years down the line when her book was finally published. We tapped into how she felt, what difference the book was going to make, how much of herself she had put into the book, who was congratulating her on the day. She then went away and wrote six reminder postcards of what that feeling was like, of where she was heading. She chose to use post-cards since she discovered that over the years she had bought a supply of postcards that held particular memories for her; she knew she would enjoy receiving them back. She gave them to someone she trusted with the request that one be posted to her every two months. The cards serve as a reminder to her of where she is heading, and she knows when she receives one it's time to celebrate, no matter where she is in her journey toward her particular dream of writing that book.

EXERCISE: Celebrating Starts Here!

Take out your journal and allow yourself some time to relax and go within. Jot down answers to the questions below. Do not analyze, go with your instincts, what stirs inside.

In what way can you celebrate who you are and who you continue to become?

- *Today?*
- *Tomorrow?*
- *Next week?*
- *Next month?*
- *Next year?*

We do not want to mislead you into thinking you must figure out what you want in the future—just see what comes up for you.

- *What will make this celebration real?*
- *What will have you commit to celebrating?*
- *What do you want people who are close to you to notice about you over the coming year?*
- *What will make that happen?*

By now you know that if you are going to make a change in who you are you don't just dream about it. Change requires preparation, choice, and action. And this is a cause for celebrating in the way that you want.

Once you have embraced the idea of celebrating, pay attention to how you feel, what your life is like. Is there a difference—are you a little more lighthearted and joyous? Are you beginning to feel this richness more often? This is where we hope we have taken you.

Having the life you want is a daily practice (it is for all of us) and each day is a new opportunity; each moment is a new chance to choose what you want. Being at peace with your choice and celebrating it, can bring more magic into your life…a life richer than you've ever imagined. Try it and see for yourself! It is *never* too late.

We hope you have enjoyed this personal workout. With this greater sense of who you are, your ability to tap into your different energies and honor your values, you are well placed to take fear and the courage to change in both hands. Dreaming is great to fill you with intentionality—action and learning make it real. *Get yourself into the driver's seat of your life—explore the choices that are uniquely yours and create your life your way!*

Bibliography

Banks, Sydney. *The Enlightened Gardener: A Novel*. Auburn, WA: Lone Pine Publishing, May 2001.

"Business Life: Macho Business Muscle Gives Itself a Feminine Makeover." *Financial Times* (May 2005).

The Coaches Training Institute. http://www.thecoaches.com. Leadership Program: http://www.thecoaches.com/leadership

Cooper, Robert K., Ph.D. "A New Neuroscience of Leadership: Bringing Out More of the Best in People." *Strategy and Leadership Journal* (January 2001). http://www.robertkcooper.com/leadership/resources/documents/Neuroscience ofLeadership.pdf

Chao, Elaine. Keynote Speech by the Secretary for Labor at the Conference on Women Entrepreneurship (March 2002). www.dol.gov/_sec/media/speeches/20020319_Women_Conf_Keynote.htm

Dench, Dame Judi, biography. http://www.tiscali.co.uk/entertainment/film/biographies/judi_dench_biog.html

Jarow, Rick. *Creating the Work You Love: Courage, Commitment, and Career*. Rochester, VT: Destiny Books, November 1995.

Jeffers, Susan, Ph.D. *Feel the Fear and Do It Anyway*. London: Century, 1987.

Johnson, Spencer, and Kenneth H. Blanchard. *Who Moved My Cheese? An Amazing Way to Deal with Change in Your Work and in Your Life*. New York: Putnam Adult, 1998.

Joseph, Jenny. *Warning: When I Am an Old Woman I Shall Wear Purple*. London: Souvenir Press, 2001. http://www.poemhunter.com/poem/warning/

Kabat-Zinn, Jon. *Wherever You Go, There You Are: Mindfulness Meditation in Everyday Life*. New York: Hyperion, 1994.

Levinson, Samuel. "Beauty of a Woman." http://halife.com/halife/beauty woman.html

McTaggart, Lynne. *The Field: The Quest for the Secret Force of the Universe*. New York: HarperCollins, April 2003.

Mills, Roger, and Elsie Spittle. *The Wisdom Within*. Auburn, WA: Lone Pine Publishing, October 2001.

Murray, Jennifer. *Broken Journey*. Norfolk, UK: Navigator Guides, 2006.

———. *Now Solo*. Edinburgh: Mainstream Publishing, 2003.

O, The Oprah Magazine.

Tandy, Jessica. Biography: http://uk.movies.yahoo.com/artists/t/Jessica-Tandy/biography-137469.html

Tolle, Eckhart. *The Power of Now: A Guide to Spiritual Enlightenment*. Novato, CA: New World Library, 1999.

Villoldo, Alberto, Ph.D. *Shaman, Healer, Sage: How to Heal Yourself and Others through the Energy Medicine of the Americas*. New York: Harmony, 2000.

Whitworth, Laura, Henry Kimsey-House, and Phil Sandahl. *Co-Active Coaching: New Skills for Coaching People Toward Success in Work and Life*. Mountain View, CA: Davies-Black Publishing, 1998.

Williamson, Marianne. *A Return to Love: Reflections on the Principles of "A Course in Miracles."* London: Aquarian, 1992.

Quotes:

http://www.micheleagnew.com/about.html

http://www.brainyquote.com/quotes/quotes/w/williamsha109527.html

http://www.quotationspage.com/quotes/

http://www.theotherpages.org/quote.html

http://womenshistory.about.com/library/qu/blqulist

Other Inspirations: Books, Movies, Websites

The Arbinger Institute, *Leadership and Self Deception: Getting Out of the Box* (San Francisco: Berrett-Koehler Publishers, Inc., 2002).

Byrne, Rhonda, *The Secret*, DVD and book (Chicago: TS Production, LLC, 2006). www.thesecret.tv

Canfield, Jack, and Mark Victor Hansen, *Chicken Soup for the Soul* (Deerfield Beach, FL: Health Communications, Inc., 1993).

Coelho, Paul, *The Alchemist: A Fable about Following Your Dream* (San Francisco: Harper San Francisco, 1995).

Gladwell, Malcolm, *Blink—The Power of Thinking Without Thinking* (New York: Penguin, 2006).

Jaworski, Joseph, Betty S. Flowers, and Peter Senge, *Synchronicity: The Inner Path of Leadership* (San Francisco: Berrett-Koehler, 1998).

Patterson, Kerry, Joseph Grenny, Ron McMillan, and Al Switzler, *Crucial Conversations: Tools for Talking When Stakes Are High* (New York: McGraw-Hill, 2002).

Payson, Eleanor D., M.S.W., *The Wizard of Oz and Other Narcissists: Coping with the One-Way Relationship in Work, Love, and Family* (Royal Oak, MI: Julian Day Publications, 2002).

Pullman, Philip, *Northern Lights: WITH Subtle Knife AND Amber Spyglass (His Dark Materials)* (New York: Scholastic Press, 2004).

Rosenberg, Marshall B., Ph.D., *Non-Violent Communication—A Language of Life: Create Your Life, Your Relationships, and Your World in Harmony with Your Values* 2nd edition (Encinitas, CA: Puddledancer Press, 2003).

Ruiz, Don Miguel, *The Four Agreements: A Practical Guide to Personal Freedom* (San Rafael, CA: Amber-Allen Publishing, 1997).

Sheets, Alan, and Barbara Tovey, *The Light With No Shadow* (San Anselmo, CA: New Equations, 2004). www.newequations.com

What the Bleep Do We Know and *What the BLEEP—Down the Rabbit Hole*, DVDs (Olympia, WA: Lord of the Wind Films, LLC, 2004). www.whatthebleep.com

White, E. B., *Charlotte's Web* (New York: HarperCollins Publishers, 1980).

If you want to find your own personal life coach, contact: International Coach Federation, www.coachfederation.org

Book Summary

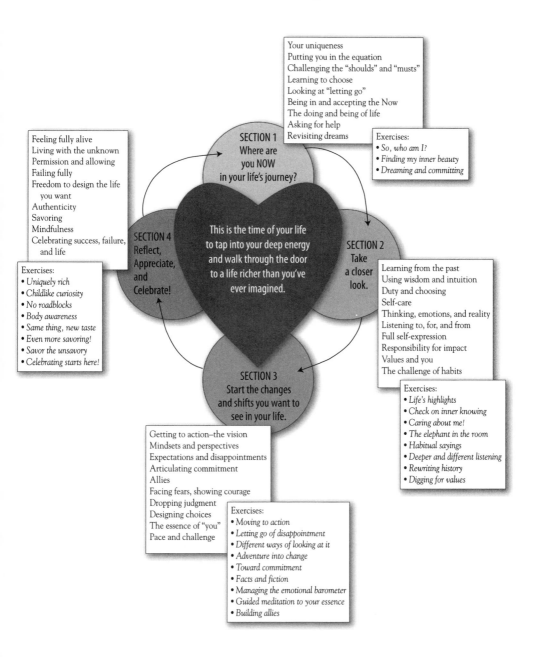

Your uniqueness
Putting you in the equation
Challenging the "shoulds" and "musts"
Learning to choose
Looking at "letting go"
Being in and accepting the Now
The doing and being of life
Asking for help
Revisiting dreams

SECTION 1
Where are you NOW in your life's journey?

Exercises:
• *So, who am I?*
• *Finding my inner beauty*
• *Dreaming and committing*

Feeling fully alive
Living with the unknown
Permission and allowing
Failing fully
Freedom to design the life you want
Authenticity
Savoring
Mindfulness
Celebrating success, failure, and life

Exercises:
• *Uniquely rich*
• *Childlike curiosity*
• *No roadblocks*
• *Body awareness*
• *Same thing, new taste*
• *Even more savoring!*
• *Savor the unsavory*
• *Celebrating starts here!*

SECTION 4
Reflect, Appreciate, and Celebrate!

This is the time of your life to tap into your deep energy and walk through the door to a life richer than you've ever imagined.

SECTION 2
Take a closer look.

Learning from the past
Using wisdom and intuition
Duty and choosing
Self-care
Thinking, emotions, and reality
Listening to, for, and from
Full self-expression
Responsibility for impact
Values and you
The challenge of habits

Exercises:
• *Life's highlights*
• *Check on inner knowing*
• *Caring about me!*
• *The elephant in the room*
• *Habitual sayings*
• *Deeper and different listening*
• *Rewriting history*
• *Digging for values*

SECTION 3
Start the changes and shifts you want to see in your life.

Getting to action–the vision
Mindsets and perspectives
Expectations and disappointments
Articulating commitment
Allies
Facing fears, showing courage
Dropping judgment
Designing choices
The essence of "you"
Pace and challenge

Exercises:
• *Moving to action*
• *Letting go of disappointment*
• *Different ways of looking at it*
• *Adventure into change*
• *Toward commitment*
• *Facts and fiction*
• *Managing the emotional barometer*
• *Guided meditation to your essence*
• *Building allies*

About the Authors

Lynn Hull, Certified Professional Co-Active Coach, Co-Active Leadership Program graduate, conducts her own coaching, consultancy, and leadership development business. Although she lived in the UK most of her life, she and her husband recently fulfilled one of their dreams and now reside in the South of France. They have one adult daughter who lives in London.

LYNN HULL

Julie Molner, Certified Professional Co-Active Coach, Co-Active Leadership Program graduate, maintains a coaching and leadership practice and lives with her husband in Michigan, USA. They have three adult children and one grandchild who also live in Michigan.

As successful career women, wives, and mothers, Lynn and Julie have experienced a wide range of change and transition in their

JULIE MOLNER

lives. When they approached the age of fifty they each started a more intensive phase of personal development and growth, which led them to make career changes as well as improvements in their personal lives. They both wanted to live their lives more fully and authentically. Filled with a renewed sense of purpose, passion, and energy, new opportunities and possibilities came their way—life became richer.

Lynn was in the UK and Julie in the state of Michigan. So why and how do two women from essentially different cultures living thousands of miles apart coauthor a book? Quite independently, their paths led them to the Co-Active Leadership Program where they met and subsequently joined forces.

Lynn and Julie share a passion to see more and more mature women living a rich life and having a positive impact on their families, communities, and the world. They found that magically (or so it seemed) their deep understanding of each other and their commitment to get their message out made it possible to move forward as coauthors. As for the "how," they used any means possible, which included a great deal of emails—not to mention flights each way across the pond.

In this book Lynn and Julie facilitate a range of powerful thinking and experiential techniques founded on psychological and spiritual principles. Their mission is to share them with other women for their benefit and their growth.

YOUR LIFE YOUR WAY

The Essential Guide for Women

Write to the Authors

Lynn and Julie request that you share how you've changed *your* life to *your* way, no matter how much or how little, by sending your story to their email address below. With your consent, it will be posted on their website to help support and encourage other women readers to design *their* life *their* way. When submitting a story, indicate how you want to be identified. For example, let them know if you want your name or initials to appear and if you want the city, state or country in which you reside to be listed. Please specify if your success stories are as a result of reading the book.

Lynn and Julie are also available for lectures, workshops, and group coaching in the United States and Europe. They would of course also be happy to consider contributing to your event anywhere else in the world.

For more information or to make a request, please visit their website or send an email.

Website: **www.essentialguideforwomen.com**

Email: **info@essentialguideforwomen.com**